FROM BRICK AND MORTAR
AND MORTAR
TO
PROSPERITY

HOW I CREATED WEALTH

PETER H PAULSEN

Peter H Paulsen/From Brick and Mortar to Prosperity Printed in the United States of America

From Brick and Mortar to Prosperity/ Peter H Paulsen -1st ed. ISBN 978-1964282008 Print Edition

LCCN 2024906924

CONTENTS

CHAPTER 1

ANGELS ON MY SHOULDERS

OVER THE YEARS, IT BUILT AND BUILT

When I was a young, successful businessman, not that many years after I immigrated to the United States from Germany, my aunt often said something that's stayed with me since. This aunt, whom we called Tanta Tieda, had herself immigrated from Germany at age 16 and settled in Iowa. She would say to me, "Peter, you have angels on your shoulders. No matter what you do, it's always great."

That was a nice thing to hear, although I don't know for sure about the angels part. I'm not pretending to be great, but I will say that, over the years, most things I've done turned out positively for me.

I firmly believe that comes from having determination and a positive attitude. And that is something anyone can embrace, if they want to.

How do you do that? By finding the silver lining, focusing on the positive, and looking to the future. My whole life, my goal has been for each day, each moment, to be incrementally better than the one before it.

I've accumulated significant wealth, but I think it's important to state that I never had an overarching goal of becoming super rich someday. Instead, my goal was simply to be better off each year than I'd been the previous year. I always gave myself a small goal, and once I accomplished it, I gave myself another one.

That perpetuated itself. Over the years, it built and built.

Using this approach, I've been extremely successful in everything I did and continue to do. I started by establishing my own masonry company when I was 22 years old. From there, I built my first housing development, consisting of eleven homes. I went on to build apartment complexes, office buildings, and even a waterfront hotel. I've owned shopping centers and started a bank. With each of these endeavors, I experienced tremendous success.

POSITIVE GOALS

Believe me, I understand that it might seem hard to dream of great success, particularly these days. So many people, especially young people, are starting off with almost nothing. But here's the thing: I, too, started with nothing. When I was a young man, I didn't have any money, period. Nobody gave me any money. Everything I've done was accomplished by using research, wisdom, and perseverance.

I've always had the ability and passion to read, learn, and continually reimagine my goals. With everything I did, I always had a positive goal, one that I had 100% certainty I could achieve.

I'm a huge believer in thinking positively. When I was a young man, I read Norman Vincent Peale's *The Power of Positive Thinking*. I also read Napoleon Hill's *Think and Grow Rich*. Over the years, I've read and re-read those books (and many, many others, including *Rich Dad, Poor Dad*, by Robert Kiyosaki), because they're enlightening and inspiring.

Beyond positive thinking, I also believe there's great power in treating others as you want to be treated yourself. I've always been very relationship-focused, whether the relationship was with a family wanting to buy a home from me, an entrepreneur seeking a loan from my bank to get a startup off the ground, or the owner of a mom-and-pop store who wanted to rent retail space in one of my shopping centers. In all those scenarios and every other, my goal has always been to build trust. And that must come from the heart and from reality. It must come from within, so people won't think you're just putting on a show. It must come from a positive outlook that you never let dwindle.

Does that mean everything in my life always went as planned? Of course not. But when something happened to me that wasn't good at the time, I never got upset about it. I knew something better would come along.

If it's not meant to be, it doesn't happen. And better comes in the door two weeks later.

ALWAYS LOOKING AHEAD

Every stage and every year, I experienced 100% improvement in my financial wellbeing, over the year before. Each time, I could have settled back and said, "I'll just coast from here." Instead, I got bored and went on to the next step.

Another key to my success is that I've always been thorough. Before beginning a new project, I read and researched obsessively. I never jumped into anything "just to see if it might work." Instead, I gathered as much information as I could, as quickly as I could, and then I made a decision. From there, I didn't look back.

To this day, that's how I work: read, research, make a decision, act on it—and anticipate a great outcome.

You have to think positively. Don't underestimate the power of positive thinking. I firmly believe that positive thinking has moved mountains for me, and it moves mountains for anyone who has that positive attitude.

WORKING FROM THE HEART

So, is it about following your heart? Partially, but you must be practical, too. I took on projects I was enthused about, but I was always looking for opportunities to make money from them. Being successful satisfies something within me. When I make an investment of any sort, it has to turn a profit. If I don't make a profit, then I'm not happy with what I'm doing.

Over the years, I found that doing things on my own, doing them my way rather than someone else's, was the most profitable method for me. For example, if you build an office building or a development of homes, by doing your own construction instead of hiring outside contractors, you're building at cost. That's where you make money.

You have to be sensible about what you do, of course. For instance, several decades ago, I bought a couple of shopping centers in Scottsdale, Arizona. At the time, that was a sensible thing to do but today, that probably wouldn't be the case. It's very difficult to make money buying a shopping center today. If you bought a new shopping center now, you'd likely only get 4% return on your investment, as cash flow. That's not very much, especially when you consider the overhead, time, and stress involved in owning a shopping center. If you built your own rather than buying an existing one, you'd probably get 25% profit—but building a shopping center is no small endeavor. By contrast, these days I spend most of my time investing in stocks. When I buy stocks, 4% is the minimum dividend (with a 20%-30% total return on investment) that I'll accept. But I don't have any overhead. I have no vacancies or tenant improvements to worry about. I have nobody wanting me to change the lightbulbs.

That's simple, common sense. I work from the heart, but my heart is driven by my mind. That's where my passion is, in those pursuits of the mind.

FOLLOWING MY OWN PATH

I might be one of a kind; I don't really know. I *do* know that I'm an individual who has always done things differently from most folks.

In the beginning, my goals were modest. When I came from Germany to the United States, I read a lot of books about wealth acquisition and real estate. My wish was to someday own several apartment buildings. I figured that if I had those buildings to own and manage, I could retire and no longer have to do much work. That was my goal, at the time.

I didn't have any idea, when I was 19 or 20, that I'd acquire enough wealth to retire quite comfortably by age 30. I also had no idea that I'd get to that age and realize that, despite my wealth, retiring was the *last* thing I wanted to do.

I never would have imagined—not at 20, not even at 30—that I'd be as successful as I am today. It was beyond my wildest dreams that I could live the way I do now. That I could be this prosperous, have everything I could possibly want, and still have plenty left over to give to charity, something I love to do through my foundation, the Peter Paulsen Foundation. It's amazing, looking back over my lifetime, to recall everything I've done and how it got me where I am today.

WHY THIS BOOK?

Everyone always asked me, "How in the world did you do all that, Peter? You didn't even go to college. So how did you get to be so smart and wealthy, when so many people can't get there?"

More importantly, they'd ask me, "How can we learn from what you did?"

This book answers both of those questions. I'll explain not only my path, but how each step I took built upon the one before it, increasing my wealth with each new plan and project. I'll discuss how, in my early years, I did it with 100% financing (explained in detail later in the book).

I'm a firm believer in education—not just classroom education, but also the lessons that life teaches us if we're willing to learn. Thus, in addition to explaining what I *did*, in this book I'll also   talk about what I *learned* along the way. My hope is that readers will be inspired by my story and will use it to build success stories of their own.

At the end of each chapter in this book is a section called "Challenge Yourself," which includes questions to ask yourself about your *own* path toward success. I encourage you to consider the questions thoughtfully, write your answers down, and use those insights to take action-steps toward achieving your goals.

I wrote this book for my children, grandchildren, and greatgrandchildren, and for anyone else who finds my story motivating and might follow my steps toward success.

I'm excited to share my journey with you, and I wish you all the best on your own successful lifetime path.

CHALLENGE YOURSELF

- What are your goals, both immediate and long term? In what ways are you currently working toward your goals?

- Do you believe positive thoughts have an impact on outcomes? Why or why not?

- Consider times in your life when you've thought positively. How did things turn out?

- Do you work from your head or your heart? If you feel unbalanced toward one or the other, what steps can you take to balance your actions between the two

CHAPTER 2

A WAR TIME CHILDHOOD (1934 – 1945)

THE SHOPKEEPER'S SON

I was born in 1934 in the small town of Schardebüll, about 120 miles north of Hamburg, Germany. Our town was in the state of Schleswig-Holstein, in Nordfriesland, which is the northern most district in Germany, very close to the Danish border. Friesland is part of Denmark, and the district where I was born is called Nordfriesland because it's so close to the border. This area had once been owned by the King of Denmark. Because we were so close to the border, there was a lot of Danish influence in the town. Many people spoke Danish, and the lifestyle was more like that of Denmark than that of central Germany. We were German by nationality, but culturally, the area I grew up in felt like it could have been in Denmark.

My father, Andreas, had a contracting business. My mother, Amanda, had a small grocery store, about half the size of a modernday 7-Eleven. Her store was attached to our house, so she was able to work in the store and raise a family at the same time. Four years after I was born, my only sibling came along, my brother, Werner.

Not long after Werner's birth, my father was drafted into the Germany army. He was sent to the front, and he never came back. He was hardly alone; every male in our town aged 15 through 60 was conscripted into the army during this time. Most of them never came back.

In our family, that left my mother alone. In the beginning, she believed my father would come home someday, and things would get better. But over time, I think she realized his return was becoming less likely. Either way, she had to take on all the responsibility of providing for our family. The silver lining is that from a very early age, I experienced the positive influence of my mother's self-sufficiency.

Our family was fortunate that we had the store. In those days, nothing was prepackaged. Everything came in bulk, and we had to weigh it out for customers on the scale, by the pound or half pound. Everything was allocated with rationing coupons. Every bulk item we sold had to match the rationing coupon, or my mother could go to jail.

From the time I was small, I was busy working in the store whenever I wasn't in school. We also had a garden, so I was responsible for helping plant and tend the crops.

In the store, I learned to use the cash register. This was how I began to understand financial strategy. I learned what everything we sold cost and what our profit would be. I became adept at ringing up a customer's order and ensuring they gave me rationing coupons in the correct amount. From early on, I had a financially oriented mind. Math and numbers came easily to me.

At the end of each month, I watched my mother pay the bills. She always took a 2% discount. Once, I asked her what that was for, and she said, "That's a rebate." We called it *rabatt* in Germany. "When you pay your bills before the tenth of the month," my mother explained, "you get a two percent discount."

For the first year or so I lived in America, I followed that philosophy. When I was getting my start, whenever I paid bills, I automatically took a 2% discount for paying the bill on time. I didn't ask; I thought it was the norm. The merchants never complained.

A DETERMINED BOY

Even as a child, I was very focused. Whether it was work or play, I'd do only one thing at a time. I'd put intense focus on the one thing, doing it as well as I possibly could.

This, I came to realize, was a different approach than a lot of people take. Many people try to multitask, which is something I've never done. I'm more successful at a task if I put all my energy into it, rather than becoming distracted by other things. I think that's just how I'm wired. Every weekday, we went to school from 8:00 AM to 5:00 PM. On Saturdays, we had a half day of school.

In August, we had two weeks of vacation from school.

As I mentioned, I was very good in math. I always got an A-plus in math, which was helpful in my future endeavors. Conversely, I wasn't the best at writing. That made sense when I was diagnosed as being dyslexic. For a while, that diagnosis bothered me. But many years later, I learned about the numerous famous, successful people who were dyslexic: Winston Churchill, Albert Einstein, Steven Spielberg, and many others. Once I realized how common it was, I didn't give it another thought. I also learned to rely on the dictionary, which helped tremendously.

It was to my advantage that, at a young age, I understood and accepted these aspects of myself: that I was a wiz at math, that I prefer doing one thing at a time, and that writing was sometimes challenging for me. Each person is unique, and if you're going to go into business for yourself, like I did, it's important to know which particular strengths *you* possess, and how you can use them to your greatest advantage. Conversely, it's important to know your challenges and explore what you can do to overcome them (or work around them).

BOMBING OF HAMBURG

Because we were close to Denmark, the war kind of passed us by. Our town was never bombed; we were too small and insignificant for the Allies to bomb us. However, in July 1943, we saw hundreds and hundreds of planes flying overhead, on their way to bomb the city of Hamburg. This happened every night for seven nights straight. The sky was lit up over Hamburg, 120 miles away. At the time, it was the heaviest aerial assault that had ever taken place in any war. Although Hamburg was south not east of us, it looked like the sun was coming up over the city. But that wasn't a sunrise; it was the 2,000-degree firestorms that resulted from the Allies dropping incendiary bombs (i.e., bombs designed to ignite fires) on Hamburg.

When the bombing was over, the casualties numbered 37,000, with another 180,000 wounded, the vast majority of them civilians. A quarter million homes were destroyed. Ninety percent of the entire city was gone.

We didn't know this at the time, but in order to plan this attack, the British Royal Air Force studied everything they knew about the London Blitz that had occurred some years earlier, during which Germany bombed London night after night. By researching the Germans' techniques, the RAF learned the most effective way to destroy a city, which was to use incendiary bombs on the neighborhoods where people (mostly factory workers) lived. This is what the Germans had done during the London Blitz, and the Allies used these same aerial bombing techniques to return fire on Hamburg.

During most of the week Hamburg was bombed, the experience didn't really frighten us. We were so far north, and the Allies had no strategic reason to bomb us. We felt relatively safe—with one notable exception. One morning when we were on our way to school, some of the fighter planes returning to England began shooting machinegun fire in our direction. They were aiming for horses that were pulling the wagons on the road. We had to dive into a ditch and take cover until they'd passed. That was absolutely terrifying.

But in general, we weren't worried for our own safety. We understood war. When you grow up during that time and in that place, it's simply part of your childhood. We didn't think much about what the wider world thought about the war or about Germany. Living in a country at war was just how things were. We had no choice but to deal with it.

We had some distant relatives in Hamburg, all of whom lost their homes. The lucky ones were evacuated. The unlucky ones died in the firestorms.

Fortunately, our close family was all nearby. We had numerous aunts, uncles, and cousins living in about a ten-mile radius. We visited with them monthly. We had to ride bicycles to visit; we didn't have a car. Before the war, my father had had a motorcycle, but it was confiscated. This was common; most cars and other vehicles were confiscated by the government. Also, gasoline wasn't available, as it was only being used for military purposes. So even if you had an automobile or a tractor—and few people did—you wouldn't be able to find any gasoline to power it.

When that happened, many people began using horses and buggies, the way previous generations did before the automobile was invented. When company visited us for a holiday or a birthday party, they'd often arrive in a buggy. This was just what people did back then, made do with what they had. When your country is at war, especially on its own soil, you have no choice. You learn to adapt.

Throughout the war, we were continually fed propaganda by the Third Reich. For example, ordinary German citizens knew little, if anything, about the London Blitz that had happened prior to the bombing of Hamburg. Hitler's propaganda was designed to convince us that Germany was being attacked for no reason.

BOYS' CLUB?

During the war, boys my age were required by law to join *Deutsches Jungvolk in der Hitler Jugend*—German Youngsters in the Hitler Youth, often abbreviated DJ. This was the arm of the Hitler Youth organization set up specifically for nineto-fourteen-year-olds. Membership in DJ was mandatory. If a boy didn't join, his parents were considered enemies of the Reich and could end up in a concentration camp.

Of course, we knew nothing about concentration camps. We learned about them later. During the war, we only knew that sometimes people were hauled away and didn't come back, but we had no idea where they went.

One time, a friend of mine made a joke about Hitler. Word got out, and the SS came to his house and picked him up. He wasn't heard from until after the war, when he returned to our town after spending years in a concentration camp. When he returned, he weighed only seventy pounds.

Hitler Youth was supposed to be like a boys' club, but in reality it was a training camp for Hitler's army. We were being trained and prepared to be sent to the front lines of the war at age 14, or even younger, if you were tall enough. At age nine, myself and other boys in my community received weekly training in how to use a rifle. By 1945, the year the war ended, we were being trained to use a bazooka gun, the weapon designed for attacking tanks at short range.

At first, I thought it was fun dealing with real ammunition and weapons. But none of us had any idea about the purpose of our training. It's possible that our parents knew, or at the very least speculated. That must have been terrifying for them, but there was nothing they could do about it. Defying the law would get our parents in trouble, and they would wind up in a concentration camp.

Nobody would talk to their kids about DJ, because you never knew who might overhear you. You didn't know if there was some sort of listening device in your house, or if someone might turn you in to the SS. Thus, nobody said a word about how bad things were. No one dared to say a word against the Reich.

Kids my age didn't really understand that we were being ruled by a dictator. We didn't comprehend the power of a man like Hitler or a government structure like the Reich. When you live within such a situation, especially at a young age, it's difficult to have perspective.

It was only later, when I moved to America, that I began to understand how precious freedom and democracy are. Since moving to the U.S., I've always stayed informed about politics. Ever since I received my U.S. citizenship, I've voted in every election. In America, I've greatly appreciated being able to vote.

A HUNGER FOR INFORMATION

Another thing I learned from the war wasn't clear to me until much later, but I was likely absorbing this lesson back then: *information is power*. In Germany at that time, because Hitler controlled all the information, he had ultimate power.

When you only have a single source for information, like we did in those days, your power is severely limited. This is one of the reasons that after the war and as I grew, I read about and researched absolutely everything that interested me. I've used my hunger for information to continually improve and generate one success after another.

All my life, I've had that hunger for information. Looking back, perhaps that's because accurate, thorough information didn't exist for me during childhood. The free flow of information we have in the U.S. is clear evidence that people are more likely to thrive and prosper when they have access to information. It's something none of us living in free countries should ever take for granted.

A BOUNTIFUL CHILDHOOD

Despite all this—the war, Hitler Youth, propaganda, and the horrifying bombing of Hamburg—Werner and I never complained. As kids, we loved what we were doing. We loved working in the store.

Our mother didn't pay us, but she'd get us new bicycles every now and then, when she could afford them.

My mother was an enterprising and resilient woman. In many ways, she was an entrepreneur. It's really because of how she raised me that I embraced that entrepreneurial spirit.

She also had a strong German work ethic. Years later, my daughter, Susan, recalled her grandmother thus: "She taught us to bake, clean, and maintain a household. When we visited her, she put us to work. Sheets had to be steam pressed; glassware had to be shined. Everything was organized just so."

Besides helping out in my mother's store, I also worked on neighbors' farms after school. I'd help the neighbors plant crops or plow fields with their horses. I found manual labor enjoyable; it was a refreshing break from the rigors of schoolwork. I didn't get paid, but I'd often have dinner with a family I'd worked with on a particular day. This was a valuable lesson in the importance of community.

As I mentioned earlier, we also planted our own crops and were able to enjoy the harvest from our garden. We produced everything ourselves. We grew all kinds of vegetables, and we canned them so we could have vegetables throughout the year, even in winter. We made our own juice from fruit trees we grew. We made our own butter, using cream from our neighbors' cows. What people have now modern-day supermarkets where you can buy anything and everything would have astounded us, back then.

Honestly, despite it being wartime, I had a good childhood. My mother was extremely capable, and she completely took the reins when my father left for the war. Werner and I never felt vulnerable or unsafe. Nor did we experience extreme hunger or poverty, the way many other people did during those times.

By today's standards, my childhood probably doesn't seem bountiful. But we didn't know anything different, and we knew that many people were suffering greatly. We felt lucky to be who we were, and to live where we did.

CHALLENGE YOURSELF

- Think back on your childhood. Who influenced you the most? What lessons did you learn that are still valuable to you today?

• What cultural or political events shaped your early years? How did they help or hinder you? How did they affect your philosophy and approach to life?

• What are your greatest strengths?

• If you have disadvantages, what changes can you make to minimize those disadvantages?

• In areas that cannot be changed (for example, dyslexia), what work-arounds can you use to maximize your strongest characteristics and most significant strengths?

CHAPTER 3

GROWING UP, GROWING AWAY (1945 – 1952)

POSTWAR GERMANY

As I mentioned previously, the community where I grew up wasn't bombed during World War II, because there was no military structure there. We were spared by virtue of being a farming community. Small cities that supported the farm industry were of no consequence to the Allies.

After the war, there were no more nightly Allied planes flying overhead to bomb Hamburg. But there wasn't much else, either. It took Germany many, many years to recover from the war.

The postwar years, after the infrastructure of the country had been demolished, were difficult for German citizens. The city of Hamburg was 95% destroyed. All other major German cities had been bombed and destroyed, too.

People lost everything. There was nothing to buy. There was no money; there was nothing going on. It would be the early 1950s before any sort of rebuilding happened.

We were no longer at war, but in our community, we lived almost as if we were, because goods were still severely rationed. Our purchases were no longer rationed by the Reich, but the British, who now occupied Germany, imposed rationing on all German civilians.

In addition to the infrastructure, much German farmland had been decimated during the war. Because of limited opportunities for growing crops and raising livestock in many parts of the country, there simply was not enough food to go around—especially when the needs of city dwellers, many of whom had lost everything, were considered. Since we lived in a farming community, people would come to our town, wanting to trade an expensive suit or leather shoes for a dozen eggs or other food supplies. We had our own chickens. The neighbor had cows, and we helped on their farm in exchange for milk and cream.

The British allowed us "half a pig." That meant we received a permit to raise one pig to be slaughtered, the meat to be shared with another family. But we cheated. We bought two little pigs and raised them without a permit, so each family could have one whole pig. The meat from one pig would last a family a year.

This was a top-secret undertaking; we could have been arrested for it. When it came time to slaughter the pigs, a butcher who was also a family member butchered them. For days, we prepared the meat for long-term storage. Everything was cooked and sealed in cans. We made our own sausage. We made everything from scratch.

The hams were cured and sent to the smokehouse, but each pig needed a permit. We had only one permit and had to bribe the butcher to put a stamp on four hams instead of two. He said, "This is the first time I've seen a pig with four hind legs." We bribed him with beer and shots of brandy. After a couple of shots of brandy, he agreed to stamp our four-legged hams.

One afternoon, four British jeeps pulled up at our house, on authority of the *Burgermeister*, or mayor, of our town. My mother thought they were there to check our permits for slaughtering hogs. She was terrified; she told me to hide the hams in a deep hole in the attic. Luckily, they were not discovered by the British. If they had been, my mother could have gone to jail.

Although we received milk and cream from the neighbor's cow, we weren't allowed to have whipping cream and butter. It had to be turned in to the British authorities. Again, my mother cheated. When the soldiers came by to do an inspection, she hid the butter and other essentials that were not allowed under the sofa.

Once, we were having a party for someone's birthday. The ladies had made a cake with whipping cream on it. The British patrol came by, and swiftly, the cake was hidden under the sofa. All the ladies sat down on the sofa, and the cake was not discovered.

Living like this, being forced to conceal food just to scrape by and take care of your family, is not ideal for anyone. This is one of the reasons that later in my life, as soon as I was able to, I began giving money to charity. Since then, I've always made as many charitable donations as I can, and over the years, I've grown my charitable giving significantly to the point that now I have a foundation for exactly that purpose. (More on that later in the book.) I know what it's like to live with so little, you do anything you can to hang onto what you've worked for. If I can help another person or family not experience that, then I'm glad to do so.

For my mother's store, we had to buy 100-pound bags of flour from a supplier, then weigh it out, one pound or half a pound, for our customers. It was all done using stamps and permits. We had to be careful, weighing everything down to the milligram, so we would not be accused of breaking the laws imposed on us by the Allies. We'd better get 100 pounds out of a 100-pound bag of flour. If even a couple of pounds were unaccounted for, my mother could go to jail, charged with selling flour on the black market.

We also had to share our living quarters. There were a lot of refugees from the cities, and we were required to make space for them in our home. Families would share a room, everyone sleeping together in that one room, mother and children. (Most families didn't have a father, as so many of them had died during the war.) In this way, several families could share one house.

In our farming community, everyone had to share their homes with refugee families. The Paulsen household was no exception. Sometimes we had as many as three other families, a dozen or more people, living in our house with my mother, Werner, and me.

I've lived in a lot of houses since then, some small, some large. I've never forgotten what it's like to have to share living quarters, to make do and help others make do, as well. From this experience, I learned that just because I can afford an enormous house doesn't mean I *need* an enormous house. In fact, my wife and I recently downsized to a smaller home, for exactly this reason. We don't have other families living with us—but we don't have a lot of unused space, either.

A CULTURED EDUCATION

I don't want to give the impression that everything was difficult and grim during those postwar years. One of my favorite things about that time in my life was learning to dance. In Germany, dance is part of the school curriculum. Students between the ages of 12 and 14 learn to dance. Those classes were mandatory for everybody, boys and girls. We were taught waltzes, tangos, and foxtrots. We were graded in dance class, just like in any other class.

Mandatory dance classes happened all over Germany, not just in my territory in northern Germany. Therefore, all German kids knew how to dance. Being an accomplished dancer would serve me well in later years, when I immigrated to the United States and socialized in German clubs with other young German immigrants. There was plenty of dancing in those clubs! (Again, this is something I'll talk more about later in the book.)

In America, schools don't have this type of mandatory dance instruction. I've observed that in this country, many women know how to dance and seem to enjoy doing it, but men are less likely to dance. I think that's unfortunate for the men. They're missing out, in my opinion.

During my school years in Germany, we also went to the symphony and opera once or twice a year. We took a chartered bus to the city of Flensburg, near the Danish border. It was about a 45-minute bus ride. All our neighbors would pile into the bus, which dropped us off for the concert or opera, then took us home when it was over.

We loved those outings, and in this way, we learned to appreciate the symphony and opera. These are lifelong lessons that remain with me, to this day.

RICHES FROM AMERICA

Another good thing that happened after the war is that we began to receive care packages several times a year from our aunts and uncles in Iowa, in the United States. My mother had two sisters, Marie and Catherine (whom we called Tante Tieda). In the 1920s, they had both immigrated to the U.S. They married two brothers, Ingwer Hansen and Chris Hansen respectively, who also had emigrated from Germany to the U.S. in the 1920s.

They'd send wonderful care packages filled with food and other goods that were otherwise inaccessible to us. The packages usually included a can of Folgers coffee, which was unavailable to buy in Germany at that time. Having coffee delighted my mother. Whenever a can arrived, she'd invite all the ladies to our home the next morning to enjoy coffee with her.

This is a great example of sharing one's "wealth"—regardless of whether the wealth is measured in thousands of dollars, or a single can of coffee. My mother received much more pleasure from sharing her coffee with others than she would have if she'd hoarded it all for herself. In the same way, I get much more pleasure from giving to charity, via my foundation, than I would if I hoarded all my money and never shared with anybody else.

APPRENTICE BRICKLAYER

I graduated from high school in June of 1949, just a few weeks before my fifteenth birthday. Because of the war, there were limited opportunities to attend college in Germany at this time, so I had to choose a profession. I wanted to be an electrician because I liked dealing with electrical work. But there were no openings in that field.

My mother found me a position as an apprentice bricklayer with a contractor. For trade work in Germany, three years of apprenticeship was required. That was true for all trades, everything from plumbers to storekeepers to mechanics. We were required to serve three years of apprenticeship from about age 15 to 18. After completing an apprenticeship, a young person either went on for more specialized training, or else began work in the field of their choosing.

For example, to become a baker, you'd have to spend three years in a bakery apprenticeship. If you wanted to specialize—for example, if you wanted to work in a confectionary shop, creating pastries— that would be another three years. After that, you would be eligible to start your own business in that field. Otherwise, you were not permitted to work in that field.

This was true before the war, too. It's always been that way in Germany. The idea was, if you put that much time into learning a profession, usually with no pay, you tended to stick with it and became proficient at your job.

During my apprenticeship, I was working on homes and remodeling farmhouses. I wasn't paid for this work; my payment was learning the skills. The apprenticeship was about twenty miles away from home, so I lived with the boss and his family. My room was a stairway closet, with a mattress on the floor. My boss had some farm animals, and in exchange for room and board, I had to take care of the animals in the morning and in the evening, as well as clean the pig sty each day. I was supposed to get five dollars extra of spending money, but he never paid me.

I didn't complain. I was just glad to get my degree as a professional journeyman bricklayer.

This experience, and others throughout my life, taught me that you don't need a college degree to be successful. For some people, that's the right path, but it's not the *only* path to success.

As with many situations, give-and-take was required. I could have complained or quit because the boss didn't pay me for the farm work. But if I'd done that, the person it would have hurt the most was me. A few years later, being a proficient mason opened doors for me that would have been closed otherwise. If I'd become disgruntled, quit, and gone home, I would have missed out on amazing opportunities just down the road.

Sometimes, you have to push through something, knowing it's a means to an end. This was one of those scenarios.

There was an additional benefit to my sticking around: as part of my apprenticeship, I was required to go to architecture school one day a month. This "requirement" was no problem for me, as I loved learning about architecture. I drew building plans to get familiar with how structures were designed and laid out. There were no computers in those days; we did everything on a drawing board. I really enjoyed those classes, and my ultimate goal turned to becoming an architect someday.

Again, learning a skill opened doors for me later on. At the time, I didn't know how things would turn out, but my apprenticeship gave me an architectural background that I was able to put to use later   in life. When I became a real estate developer, I designed and drew plans for most of the houses, apartment complexes, and commercial buildings that I developed. This saved me a lot of money on architectural work, and my buildings were designed exactly as I wanted them to be. Additionally, I truly enjoyed that creative outlet, and I found it very rewarding.

The only thing I couldn't do was the structural engineering. I

wasn't trained to do that, and structural integrity is vital. So, I always hired that work out to a structural engineer. In Germany, to be an architect, first you had to be in the workforce as either a carpenter or a bricklayer for two years. Then, you had to go to more school, followed by working for two years as a journeyman architect. They were very thorough there. They didn't want architects drawing up plans that were physically impossible to build.

It was a lot of work, but that career path intrigued me. I began to explore the possibility of continuing my education in Germany, with the goal of someday becoming an architect.

But as it turned out, around the time my apprenticeship ended, my life took a very different path—in the form of an uncle who arrived from America for a visit.

What was *that* all about? In the next chapter, I'll explain.

CHALLENGE YOURSELF

•   What sacrifices did you have to make or what challenges did you face as a youth? What did those experiences teach you?

•   What aspects of your high school education do you remember most? How have those experiences shaped your adult life?

•   If you have (or are currently pursuing) a post-high school certificate or degree, what made you choose the path you did? If you could go back and do it again, would you choose the same path?

•   Think about times in your life when you might have considered giving up but didn't. What made you push through? How can you use that attitude to push through any current challenges you have?

•   What skills do you possess? If you're not using your skills to their greatest potential, how can you make changes to capitalize on what you do best?

CHAPTER 4

A NEW LIFE IN AMERICA (1952 – 1954)

A STEPFATHER

In 1952, my Uncle Ingwer from America, whom I mentioned in the previous chapter, came to visit. Previously, he'd been married to my mother's sister, my Tante Marie. But Tante Marie died of a heart attack at only 49 years of age.

I don't know if Uncle Ingwer came over to Germany specifically to marry my mother, but that's what happened. That sort of thing wasn't unusual, in those times. My uncle needed a wife to help him on his farm in Iowa. My mother wanted to move her family to America, for a better life and more opportunities for her two sons. Uncle Ingwer and my mother got along well, so there was no reason not to marry and improve the situation for themselves, as well as for Werner and me.

After they married, my mother was able to get a visa for herself immediately, so she closed up her shop, and she and Uncle Ingwer left for the United States. But Werner and I had to wait three months to get a visa clearance. During that time, we stayed with relatives in Germany.

Even back then, I had a business-oriented mind. I was looking forward to my move to America, but I wasn't going to sit around idly while we waited for the visa clearance. I was done with my apprenticeship, but we had three months to spare. I was working as a bricklayer for a construction company, but I had some free time, too. So I went to a lumber company and bought wood to build milking stools. I sold my milking stools to local farmers. I had to keep busy, and I wanted to make money.

I've always had the profit picture in my mind, ever since I can remember. Even back then, I knew I wanted to be a businessman one day. For three months, I had a profitable little business as a milking stool craftsman and salesman.

ACROSS THE ATLANTIC

Finally, our visa clearance came through. In May of 1952, Werner and I boarded the SS *Italia* in Hamburg, headed for New York City. The ship stopped in England, France, and Halifax, Canada.

The trip was around ten or fifteen days. I was 17, just about to turn 18. My brother was 13. Nowadays, it might seem strange for two teenagers to take a long trip like that without an adult, but back then, it was common for youth to travel alone. Many families did whatever they had to do to immigrate to the U.S.

I was in charge of the money, but we didn't have much of it. I'd received a loan from Uncle Ingwer, but I knew I'd have to pay it back. I was so tight with money that the only time I spent anything on board the SS *Italia* was to shell out five dollars for rental of lounge chairs, allowing us to sit on the deck in the sun. Our sleeping quarters and all meals were included in our passage. There were other fun things we could have spent money on, but I refused. Werner wasn't happy with me about that, but since I was the big brother, I was in charge.

There were numerous Germans on board. There were plenty of young people, not just from Germany, but also from France, England, Poland all over Europe. We were happy to be on this adventure together. We exchanged stories, played cards, and talked all day because we had nothing else to do. We also sang a lot. Some of our fellow passengers had musical instruments to accompany the singing. Overall, the trip was both relaxing and exciting.

Crossing the ocean toward a new, unknown life taught me that you have to be ready for anything. As I mentioned previously, I'd started to think about becoming an architect in Germany. But I knew my opportunities in postwar Germany would be limited, for both education and employment. Also, I didn't want to live a continent away from my mother and brother. So instead, I set my sights on a new life in a new country. I was ready to take on whatever my future held.

NEW YORK, NEW YORK

Before we left Germany, we'd had all our immunizations and taken care of everything else necessary for immigration. It was pretty straightforward to arrive in New York and disembark. Our mother had arranged for a German woman to pick us up at the boat terminal. It's a good thing she did, because we didn't speak any English and would have had a hard time getting around on our own.

Werner and I didn't stay long in New York, but we did have one experience that stands out. We went into a restaurant because it was lunchtime, and we wanted a meal. Not knowing what to order, we decided to play it safe and go for a piece of pie. We ordered what we thought was apple pie off the menu. But when our plates were set before us, it didn't taste like apple pie at all. It turned out to be chicken pot pie. We were so disappointed! That was a good reminder to us that we had a lot to learn about our new country, starting with not ordering anything off a menu that was written in a language we didn't know.

The German lady took Werner and me to the airport in New York. We flew to Chicago, another very exciting experience, my first airplane ride. A few years later, it would be commonplace for travel between Europe and the United States to be primarily by airplane. But I'm glad our first flight was short, only two hours. It introduced me to the experience on a modest scale, although air travel didn't feel modest at the time to Werner and me.

Our mother and Uncle Ingwer met us at the airport in Chicago, and from there, we drove to Clinton, Iowa, where Uncle Ingwer owned a small farm.

As an aside, I always called my stepfather "Uncle Ingwer," until I had kids of my own. After that, we all referred to him as "Grandpa."

THE HEARTLAND OF AMERICA

Uncle Ingwer had a small farm in Iowa, about eighty acres. A person couldn't get rich owning a farm that size, but you could make a decent living from it. Uncle Ingwer had one son, my cousin, who was also now my step-brother. But he was older and had his own farm.

For my first three months in America, I worked on Uncle Ingwer's farm and other nearby farms. I bailed hay and helped the farmers in exchange for room and board. This was a good way to adjust to a new country without having to make too many changes all at once. I knew farm work and was comfortable with it. And my uncle and all the other farmers and farmhands spoke German, so I was able to communicate easily with everyone. I knew I'd need to learn English in order to become successful in the United States, but it was a relief not to have to take it on immediately, just to get by.

My aunt, Tanta Tieda, had sponsored my journey to America. Tanta Tieda is also the aunt who, years later, would say that I have angels on my shoulders. She was very helpful once I arrived in the States. She and Uncle Chris had eight kids, all American born, and they lived nearby. That part of Iowa was (and still is) a lot like Northern Germany—rural, tight-knit communities where everyone knows each other, and many are related to one another.

Even though she had a huge family of her own, Tanta Tieda was loving, supportive, and encouraging toward me and everyone. She never said a mean word and always took an interest in other people's ideas, dreams, careers, and hobbies. She had a way of making everyone around her feel special. Tanta Tieda taught me, by example, that kind words and actions go a long way.

After I'd been in America a few months, my mother found a German contractor who offered me a position as a bricklayer. Back in Germany, I'd passed my examination and graduated as a master bricklayer/mason, so I had a German journeyman bricklayer/mason card. That might not have meant much to an American contractor, but for a fellow German, it showed him what my education and experience were. Again, I didn't yet speak English, but at that company, they spoke both German and English. They were happy to work with me on my English.

To take the job, I had to leave my mother and Uncle Ingwer's place. I moved to Durant, Iowa, a small town about sixty miles southwest of Uncle Ingwer's farm. I lived in the basement of a family's house. I rented the basement, which had a bedroom and a bathroom.

For lunch, I always packed myself a sandwich. But because I had no way of cooking in my basement accommodations, I often went to a restaurant in the evening to get dinner. I still didn't speak much English, and I couldn't read the menu. The first time I went there, I recalled my experience in New York with the chicken pot pie. This time, I didn't want to take any chances. So, in my halting English, I asked the waitress to help me order. She didn't understand me, and she called over another waitress. Eventually, I had about five waitresses standing around me, trying to figure out what I wanted to eat.

I said (as best I could), "I want what that person has over there. What is that?"

They looked where I was pointing, and then they nodded and brought me a plate that was the same as that of the man I'd pointed at. It was some sort of roast beef. It was very good, and as a result, I ordered that same dinner every night for the next month. I didn't want to take a chance on food I didn't understand.

I think this goes back to my methodical nature. It wasn't that I lacked a sense of adventure. I loved trying new things; still do. But I was also practical. I was trying to save up enough money to buy a car, and I certainly didn't want to waste it on food I might not like. There would be plenty of time, I reasoned, to try different American foods once my mastery of English was higher—and once I had more money to spare. I stayed in the basement place for six months, but then another family who learned that I was from Germany needed some help, so they rented me a room in their house. I was given room and board in exchange for a fee that I paid for out of my earnings. That family also taught me more English. Additionally, I arranged for a schoolteacher to tutor me in English in the evenings. I was grateful for the instruction, and I learned quickly. Eventually, I was able to order off a menu with no problem at all!

AN HONEST DAY'S PAY

At my job, I had one person who helped me. He was called the hod carrier. His job was to bring me bricks and hand them to me as I laid them. The hod carrier, sometimes called a "hoddy," carries bricks and other materials in a three-sided box with a long pole, called a hod. They can rest the loaded hod on their shoulders as they carry it.

Being a hoddy is hard work, but it's basic unskilled labor. I was the professionally trained bricklayer; my hod carrier was just the helper.

One day, I asked him what he was getting paid. "A dollar and thirty cents an hour," he told me.

I was getting a dollar an hour! That made no sense to me. I went to my boss and asked, "How come my hoddy gets more? In Germany, a bricklayer gets paid more money than the hod carrier."

I asked for a raise, and I got it. I think it's important to always ask for what you're worth. You need to make sure you have a good case for it, of course, but you should never let anyone take advantage of you.

I worked for that contractor for two years. He was a nice German man, with a family at home. I understood him, and he understood me. By this time, I'd learned how to drive, so he let me borrow a company truck to go to farms and do repair work on my own.

He'd also sometimes send me out, as a representative of the company, to fix things. That was good for the company and good for me. He trusted me because I was able to do the work without supervision.

In this way, I began building my reputation, and I continued to advance my skills. I was still young, and I knew I had a lot yet to learn if I wanted to be successful someday. I was willing to work hard as long as I was being paid fairly for the work, and I welcomed every opportunity that my boss and others gave me.

If you want to succeed, it's essential to be willing to work hard and take on opportunities that come your way. From the outside, it might appear as if many successful people were just born that way, and everything simply fell into their laps. But that's rarely the case. Almost everyone I've ever known who made it big started out small, worked hard, and built one success on top of another. And I'm no exception.

AMERICAN POLITICS

Early on in my time working for the German contractor in Durant, the United States was getting ready for the 1952 presidential election. The candidates were Dwight D. Eisenhower, the Republican, versus Adlai Stevenson, the Democrat. I wasn't yet a citizen, so I couldn't vote. Nonetheless, I was curious about American politics.

I asked my boss, "What's the difference between the Democrats and the Republicans?"

"Well," he said. "The Republicans are more for the businesspeople, and the Democrats are more for the working people."

"Very well," I replied. "Then I will be a Republican, because I'm going to be a businessman someday."

I was pragmatic. I always have been, my entire life. That's just part of who I am.

CHALLENGE YOURSELF

• What big adventures have you had? What adventures would you *like* to have? How can you work to make those dreams into reality?

• Have you experienced life outside the community where you were born and/or raised? What did you notice that was different? What was the same?

• What family members or friends have been encouraging of your dreams? In turn, how can you support the dreams of others around you?

• What is the hardest job you've ever had? What did you like and/or not about it?

• Have you ever had to ask for a raise? How did you ask? Were you successful?

• What are your politics? Do your politics reflect your values in life?

CHAPTER 5

THE GERMAN KID (1954 – 1959)

MY FIRST CAR

As I mentioned in the last chapter, when I lived alone in Durant, I often ate dinner at a particular restaurant. The restaurant owner had a 1946 Pontiac that he kept in the lot outside his place. It had a "For Sale" sign on it. I said to myself, "Someday, I'm going to buy that car."

The restaurant owner said he'd take six hundred dollars for the Pontiac. The car was well maintained but it wasn't new, so that was a fair price.

Within six months, I had enough money saved up to buy that '46 Pontiac. It was easy to save; I didn't spend much money on anything anyway. I didn't go to the movies, because I couldn't understand much of what I saw and heard there. And as I mentioned previously, I always ordered the same meal at the restaurant, because I didn't want to waste money on food I potentially wouldn't enjoy.

The Pontiac cost me my entire savings. At that time in my life, I'd never heard of a car loan. But even if I had, I wouldn't have wanted one. It felt good to be able to buy the car, free and clear.

That's something I've always done since: only bought cars that I could afford. Of course, over the years as I became more successful, I could afford nicer cars. But I never spent more on a car than I could reasonably afford. A car is a depreciating asset; it's very rare to make money when you sell one. Therefore, I advise being sensible about cars. Yes, most of us need one to get around, but if you're trying to build your wealth and success, it's important to be practical about items like a car.

My '46 Pontiac got me around just fine. I was proud of myself for saving up, and very proud of my car.

QUAD CITIES

I learned that in the Quad Cities, bricklayers were making three dollars an hour. So after I'd been in Durant for a couple of years, I told my boss I was quitting, because I planned to go work in a big city for higher pay.

He said, "Not a good idea, Peter. Here in Durant, you can always start your own business someday. You could never do that in a big city."

"Well," I said, "I'm going anyway."

I wasn't about to argue with him, but honestly, I didn't agree with him. I think he wanted me to stay in Durant because I was a hard worker and a skilled bricklayer. But, as he'd mentioned, it *was* my goal to start my own business. And despite what my boss in Durant said, I firmly believed I could do that in a larger city.

All my life, even back in Germany, I'd observed that owning property and running a business seemed to be the keys to success. I looked up to successful people; they seemed to have a good life. As a result, I got the idea—probably subconsciously at first, but later as something I thought about all the time—of having my own business.

I knew I'd need capital to start a business. If I could make more than twice the pay in the Quad Cities as I could in Durant, I'd reasonably be able to save up enough to start a business sooner, pro-vided I kept my living expenses low. It just made economic sense.

The Quad Cities is a region straddling the Mississippi River, with the Rock River flowing into it. Davenport, Iowa; Rock Island, Illinois; and Moline, Illinois have always been part of the area, originally called the Tri Cities. Later, two other municipalities were added, East Moline and Bettendorf. There seems to be some controversy over which of the two newcomers turned the area from the Tri Cities into the Quad Cities (and never did it become the Quint Cities), but I'll leave it for others to argue that point.

Regardless, for me the area represented a "big city." When I moved to Moline in 1954, the population of that city alone was about 32,000 people. Compare that with Durant (just over 1,000 in the 1950 census), and you can see why Moline felt like a big city to me.

My first day there, I drove up to every construction site I could find. At each one, I asked the boss or foreman if they were interested in hiring a bricklayer. Finally, the owner of one company said, "Yes, we need a bricklayer for our houses."

The company was called Hillbloom & McGill. I became their only bricklayer.

THE FIREPLACE BUSINESS

I happily settled into my new life. I met a German family and received room and board from them. They also helped me continue working on my English. I was getting much better, but the family members corrected me when I said something wrong. Even though I was speaking English, my mind automatically went to the German alphabet, pronouncing letters the German way. The family would tell me, "Peter, that's not the right way to say it. You've got to say it this way." They'd pronounce it the right way, and I'd repeat it, until it began to feel natural to me.

If you want to learn something, you must be willing to accept corrections. I had to be humble about learning English. If I'd been arrogant about it, always insisting I was right, then I wouldn't have learned English as quickly as I did.

For about eighteen months, I worked for Hillbloom & McGill. They were very good to work for. I was 20 years old and making the promised three dollars an hour, which was a good wage for a young worker like me. I was satisfied with my situation.

In the evenings, after I finished my day job at Hillbloom & McGill, I did quite a bit of side work. The first side project I did was for a John Deere executive. John Deere was (and still is) headquartered in Moline. The company was founded in 1836 by a man named John Deere, who developed a plow with highly polished surface. Being on the banks of the Mississippi River, Moline provided a great location for the company, which over the years expanded its product line of farming equipment.

John Deere has always been an excellent company to work for; they treat their employees very well. These days, they have a showplace in downtown Moline, displaying their products. If you go there, you'll see tractors that are twenty feet tall, combines ten feet tall and twenty feet wide.

The John Deere executive and his wife needed a fireplace built in their home. I didn't know how to build a fireplace, so I had to research it. I learned that it's a very delicate business, building a fireplace and chimney. You have to understand how smoke travels in a back chimney downward, and upward in the front. You must make sure the fire box and flue are proportioned correctly. There has to be a smoke shelf, which is a shelf above the damper that keeps the cold air downdraft from dropping down into the fireplace, thus preventing smoke from entering the room. If the fireplace and chimney are not built correctly, smoke billows into the room, rather than drafting up the chimney.

Some chimneys were three stories: a fireplace in the basement, one in the living room, and one in the master bedroom, all composed of brick. Back then, of course, they were all wood-burning fireplaces. Gas fireplaces hadn't come into vogue yet.

I learned everything I could, and I spent my evenings after work building the John Deere executive's fireplace. When it was complete, he and his wife had a cocktail party. Everyone asked, "Who did your fireplace?"

"The German kid," the executive told his friends.

"We must get him for our fireplace, too," was the reply.

And on and on it went. My reputation built, and I got offers for more brickwork than I could have ever imagined.

I told everyone about my side work for evenings and weekends. I received lots of referrals. I'd do a piece, and word would spread. By this time, my English was much improved. I talked to everybody about how I was a bricklayer, and if they needed any work done or knew someone else who needed brickwork, let me know.

For my evening jobs, I didn't work by the hour. I priced the entire job. I'd give the customer a price for finishing a fireplace or doing some brickwork along their house. My prices were fair, but I didn't shortchange myself. I knew I was providing premium work, and my customers knew it, too, and were willing to pay for it.

I also joined the Mason Contractors Association to better understand what business was like. I asked questions, listened to what was said, and learned from other contractors. After a year, they named me president of the Mason Contractors Association.

Not bad for a German kid who'd only recently become fluent in English!

THE BRICKLAYER TAKES A BRIDE

In Iowa and Illinois at that time, there were hundreds of German immigrants, many of us young adults. Most had immigrated after the war, like I did. There were a lot of young kids like myself that I could hang out with.

Because there were so many young Germans, the cities in these areas were prime locations for German clubs and dance halls. One such club was called the Nordfriesland Club, named after Nordfriesland, the province where I was born and raised. It was in the Nordfriesland Club that I met a young woman named Elke.

In 1954, when Elke and I met, I was 20. She was 16. We began dating, and soon, things turned serious.

I wanted to ask Elke to marry me, but before I did that, I needed to make sure we'd have a nice house to live in. As a result of my side jobs building fireplaces, and because I lived frugally, I was able to save up my money and purchase a building lot in Moline. The lot cost $2,500. It was an end lot that nobody else wanted. It wasn't the fanciest location in town, but it was all I could afford.

My next task was to design my house and floor plan. For this, the skills I'd learned in architectural classes in Germany came in handy. Plus, by that time I'd helped build so many houses, I'd developed a natural aptitude for how a home should flow.

I took my sketches to a lumber company. A draftsman there drew up formal architectural plans for me. They did this at no charge if you bought the lumber for your project from that lumber company.

Next, I went to a savings and loan. I had learned from the builders I worked for what was involved in getting a loan.

"I need a construction loan," I told the loan manager. "I have a lot, purchased outright."

"How much do you need?" she asked.

I had calculated my costs. Since I was doing my own brickwork and much of the other work on my house, the budget was reasonable. I told her my budget, and I said, "I want to borrow seventy-five percent for construction costs."

"That's what we do," she said. And I got my 75% loan based on economic value. At that point, I proposed to Elke, and she said yes. The house plans that the lumber company drew up included the two-car garage I'd sketched. But on their plans, it was only seventeen feet deep. I told them, "This is not going to work. My current car will fit fine, but someday, I'm going to be able to afford a Cadillac. I need my garage to be at least twenty feet deep."

They changed the plans to include a twenty-foot-deep garage for my future Cadillac. This is a lesson in thinking ahead. I didn't want to have to build a new garage or a different house in a few years, just because the car I wanted wouldn't fit in my home's garage. Instead, I thought ahead a few years and planned for that future scenario. This cost me a few extra dollars of construction costs, but it saved me quite a bit of money in the long run.

I built my home in my spare time. It was a beautiful home, all brick on the outside. When it was almost finished, I told Elke, "We're not getting married until the house is done." The holidays were coming, and I refused to spend the first Christmas with my new wife in a boring house.

The Moline Dispatch heard about me building my own house in my spare time. They came out and took a picture for a New Year's feature about what various Moline residents were looking forward to in 1956. The picture was captioned "Young Couple's Dream," and it showed Elke standing by the sink in our almost-completed kitchen, with me in my work apron, hammer and trowel in my hands, in the doorway behind her. The caption talked about how I'd built the house in my spare time, until the next side project came along. It also mentioned that Elke and I had both come to the U.S. from Germany.

We bought quality furniture from a furniture store in Moline, Illinois. Because we bought everything from the one store, we got all the furniture at a great discount.

I completed the house on December 15, 1955. Elke and I got married the very next day. We moved in, and we were in seventh heaven.

A BUSINESS IS BORN

One day, a John Deere executive called me and said, "Peter, we heard about your work. You did work for our friends; you built their fireplace."

"Yes," I said.

"We have a house we're building," he went on. "The house is framed, but it needs bricks on the outside. The material is all there, but the bricklayer doesn't show up for work when he's supposed to. Can you give me a price to finish our house?"

I thought about how I'd built my own home. I knew I could do the job he asked, so I said, "Yes, I can do that." I drove over, and since I've always been skilled with math, I calculated each brick yet to be laid, then multiplied that by the price I found when I researched what people were paying other contractors for this type of work.

It was a three-story house in the back and two stories in the front, brick all around. I knew that if I won the bid, I'd have to quit Hillbloom & McGill, because it was a six to eight-month job, not something I could do in the evenings.

I said to myself, "If I'm going to quit my job over this, I've got to have more than a hundred percent profit. The calculation I've come up with might not be enough." I decided to bid it so high that if I didn't get the job, I'd be fine with that—and if I did get it, I'd make enough money to cover me until the next project came along.

So, I bid it at 300% profit. And I got the job.

The executive gave me some advance money for this project. With that, I bought a used pickup truck and some tools, and I hired one laborer to help me.

I told my boss at Hillbloom & McGill, "Mr. McGill, I'm quitting. I'll give you two weeks' notice, but I have to quit because I'm starting my own mason contracting business."

Mr. McGill said, "I like your work, Peter. I don't want to hire another bricklayer." He went on, "Here are five home plans. Why don't you give me a bid on all the basement brickwork?"

I said fine and told him I'd get back to him with a bid. Then I made my calculations. And again, I said to myself, "I can't be the low bidder, because if I'm the low bidder they're going to say, 'Look at the ignorant immigrant from Germany.' I have to be five percent higher and ten percent better in quality."

So that's how I bid those masonry jobs, and I was awarded all that work.

Using a printing company, I had yard signs made up. Every time I did a project—house, basement, fireplace, anything—I put a sign out front that said, "Masonry by Peter Paulsen." Sometimes there'd be ten such signs on one block.

I got more damn work than I could imagine. It was too much for my single employee and myself, so I began to hire others, too. Within six months, I had six masons working for me.

Around this time, my mother called to ask what was going on. I told her I'd gone into business for myself.

But she already knew. She said, "I'm not sure that's a good idea, Peter." Turned out she'd explained my plans to a man she knew, who also had been a bricklayer and started his own masonry business.

She said, "This man told me, 'Tell Peter not to start. I started, and I failed. My brother started, and he failed.'"

"Well," I told my mother, "I'm starting anyway."

You know what happened? Within a year, the man who told my mother it wasn't a good idea to start my own business became one of my employees.

I share this story to remind you that business ownership isn't for everyone. Turned out that man had an alcohol problem. No wonder he didn't succeed in business.

This is a good reminder that if you want to be an entrepreneur, you must look at every aspect of your life—your skill set, your temperament, your lifestyle—and decide if entrepreneurship might work for you. If that man had been honest with himself, he wouldn't have started his own business. Instead, he would have focused on doing something about his alcohol problem.

BEING THE BOSS

As owner of Masonry by Peter Paulsen, I'd start my day at five in the morning, getting everything ready for my workers. The bricklayers would arrive at 8:00 and work all day. At 5:00, they went home, and I spent another hour cleaning up, so we'd be ready for the next day's work.

I had masons, bricklayers, and hod carriers. That was it. I didn't hire extra people that I didn't need. With my math skills, I did all my own accounting. And because my masonry work was well known in Moline, I didn't have to advertise a lot to get jobs. Those yard signs and my reputation did most of the advertising work for me.

Just as Elke and I were in seventh heaven in our home and marriage, I also was in seventh heaven running my business. I made more money than I ever could have imagined.

Was it daunting, running my own business at age 21? Not really, but I think that's because of my personality and drive. Keep in mind, many people are scared to strike out on their own—or, as I mentioned above, maybe they just don't have the right personality for it.

SOLE PROPRIETORSHIP

I started my masonry contracting business as a sole proprietor, the only owner of my company. When I started the company and began building homes, several carpenters approached me, wanting to be my partner. They proposed that we could bid together on projects, as a single company. We'd be one construction company, they said. They'd do the carpentry while I did the masonry.

I said, "The thing is, I like to work—a lot. And I worry that I'll be doing all the work, and you'll be taking a couple hours for lunch every day. So, thank you, but no. I don't want to be partners."

About a year after I started my company, Mr. McGill, from Hillbloom & McGill, asked me to come in for a meeting. He and his partners wanted to make me a 33% partner of their construction company.

Again, I said, "Thank you, but I don't think so." I respected Mr. McGill, but I didn't want to be business partners with him, or anybody else.

This isn't to say that partnerships don't work for other entrepreneurs. Again, it's about knowing yourself. I knew back then, and still know now, that I work best on my own. Other people work better with partners. It's a matter of looking deeply into yourself and deciding what's right for *you*.

SOCIAL AND FAMILY LIFE

I was busy running my company, but I still enjoyed my family and my leisure time. Elke and I were very close with our German community. We still belonged to the Nordfriesland Club. Many of our friends were also in the club; the majority came from that same general area of Germany. We stayed active in the club as a young married couple.

We did a lot of dancing at the Nordfriesland Club and other German clubs. Once, when Guy Lombardo came to Moline, he had a big to-do at a local ballroom (not a German club). Elke and I went. And everybody said, "What are you doing here? You kids should be on the beach." We were the only young people in the ballroom—everyone else was between 40 and 80 years old. But we loved the music and loved ballroom dancing because we'd been raised with it. We tore up the dance floor that night!

Most of my friends came over from Germany around the same time I did. They were bricklayers, electricians, carpenters, and farmers. They were happy with their lives, but few of them ran their own businesses, the way I did.

Elke and I became parents in 1957, with the birth of our first daughter, Veronica. Our middle daughter, Susan, followed in 1958. Lisa, our youngest daughter, came along in 1960.

U.S. CITIZENSHIP

From the time I arrived in the United States, I knew I wanted to become a citizen of this country. The U.S. provided me with so many opportunities and advantages, I saw no reason why I'd ever want to return to Germany to live permanently there.

I became a citizen in 1957. To obtain citizenship, I had to go to classes and study the Constitution of the United States. I had to know who the first four presidents were. I also had to memorize the names of at least four other past presidents. Besides taking classes, at that time a person had to wait for five years before taking the citizenship test. You had to be a useful member of the community, pay your taxes, and stay out of trouble. When the five years were up, and you'd done all your studying, you had to pass a citizenship test. If you passed, you were accepted as a citizen.

I was accepted for U.S. citizenship the same year my first daughter was born. Both events marked proud moments in my life.

Everyone had to wait the same five-year period. Elke had arrived in the U.S. two years after I did, so she received her citizenship two years later, in 1959.

Elke and I were feeling very good about our lives. We had our family, and I had my successful business.

We were young Americans, living the American dream.

CHALLENGE YOURSELF

• Do you remember your first car? What was it, and how did you pay for it? If you could go back to that time, would you still make the same choice? Why or why not?

• Have you ever "struck out on your own"? If so, what made you decide to do that? Today, how do you feel about the decision?

• What have your job-hunting experiences been like? Have you ever approached a company or entered a business establishment and asked for a job, even if none was advertised? If not, how would you feel about doing that?

• Are you considering starting a business? What type of business will it be? Will you have a partner or be a sole proprietor?

• How do you balance your personal and professional lives? If you feel these two aspects of your life aren't in balance, what changes can you make to balance them more evenly?

CHAPTER 6

FROM THE GROUND UP (1959 – 1962)

DREAMING BIG

By the late 1950s, business was booming for my masonry company. During that time, there was a great deal of construction in the Quad Cities, and I never ran out of projects to bid on. My income had doubled and then doubled again.

It was gratifying to see my business flourish, but I had an ambition to do even more. I just needed to determine what that "more" would be and learn how to do it.

I came across a concise but informative book, only about sixty pages long. It was written by someone in Texas, a man involved in real estate. It discussed apartment-building development and ownership. The book's author contended that in the future, there would be great demand for apartments, especially luxury apartments that gave people a nice lifestyle without the hassles of owning a house. He explained how to build wealth by owning apartment buildings.

I wish I still had that book, or at least could remember its title and author. I read it so many times, my copy became dilapidated. Eventually, with all the moving around I did, the book was misplaced.

But it certainly got me thinking. I began to dream about getting into the apartment building business. I figured that if I eventually owned enough apartments, I would no longer have to work on a daily basis. I knew it would likely take years to build up to this level, but that was my dream, being able to semi-retire at a young age.

The book explained how 75% financing for investment property works, by getting a construction loan and permanent loans. The author explained how you could complete any project with only 25% down. Because I did my own masonry and other construction work, I figured I wouldn't even need the 25% down. I could simply build for 25% less. All I needed was an appraisal that came in at the amount the bank needed to get the loan in place.

Coming across that book was serendipitous. Remember, there was no internet in those days. There were no websites or search engines that automatically plugged in your interests and came up with suggestions of what to read, what to watch, what to listen to. If a particular subject interested you and you wanted to read about it, you went to the library or a bookstore. If you weren't sure what you were looking for, you asked the bookseller or librarian for suggestions, hoping they'd be able to help you find the information you needed. You also might ask around among your friends and colleagues, to see if anyone could recommend appropriate resources.

I don't recall how I came across that book, any more than I recall its title or author. That experience demonstrates that sometimes you're simply in the right place at the right time. It happens to everyone, whether we notice it or not. The key is to take note of it and use it to your advantage.

So many people let opportunities slip by. I never did that, which I believe is another element of my success.

After I read that small volume about apartment development and ownership, I began reading every book on real estate and financing that I could get ahold of. I wanted to learn how to leverage my assets and abilities to make a profit—to build my wealth, as the apartment building book said.

All of that was my dream. I've always been a big believer in dreams. No matter what you want to do, you've *got* to have a dream, the bigger the better, in my opinion. If you can't dream it, you can't get there.

It was around this time that I also read, for the first time, *The Power of Positive Thinking* by Norman Vincent Peale and *Think and Grow Rich* by Napoleon Hill. Those books, too, inspired me, and I returned to them over and over. They helped me dream big.

AN INVESTMENT OPPORTUNITY

Soon thereafter, another serendipitous event occurred: my mother sold her house and shop in Germany. From the proceeds of the sale, Werner and I each received $4,000 cash. My brother wanted to build his dream house, so he spent his $4,000 on a very nice plot of land.

But I had other ideas. I approached the son of a lot developer who owned eleven lots in a beautiful subdivision. It was close to shopping and other amenities. I'd done masonry work in that subdivision, so I was very familiar with the area. The eleven lots were worth $4,000 each, $44,000 in total.

The son handled sales for his father's company. I said to the son, "I'd like to buy all eleven lots from you. I have four thousand dollars that I can give you as a down payment. I plan to get a construction loan to develop the lots, but I can write you a check today for four thousand dollars, as a down payment."

"Let me think on it," he said. "And I'll talk with my father about it." The next day, he came back to me and said, "I talked to my father.

Because you've got such a good reputation, we trust you. My dad says you've got a deal."

This situation reminded me of something that happened when I was about eight years old, back in Germany. There was a fair in a town several miles away. My mother gave me the German equivalent of five dollars and sent me off to the fair for the day. I had to walk there and back, but I didn't mind.

I spent all day at the fair, and when I got home that evening, I still had all my money.

"Why do you still have your money?" my mother asked. "Didn't you have any fun at the fair?"

"I had a great time at the fair," I told her. "When I got there, I went to the office of the fairgrounds people and talked to the manager. I asked if they needed somebody to help the little children on and off the seats of the carousel. They agreed, so I did that for a while. That got me into the fair for free and got me rides on the carousel for free. So, I still have my money *and* I had fun at the fair."

My experience with the $4,000 I received from my mother's real estate sales wasn't all that different. Instead of spending it all on one thing, I found a way to do the things I wanted to do *and* make that money grow into something bigger.

In Moline, with my modest investment of $4,000, I determined that I would build homes that fit the neighborhood, which was upper middle class. At the same time, I wanted to build something different from all the other builders. I'd build all brick on the outside, which no one else in that area was doing at that time. In order to get a brick home, people had to have it custom built, and most people didn't want to build their own house. They wanted to buy a house already completed, so they'd know what they were getting. I also planned to use copper plumbing rather than galvanized pipes because copper was quality.

Again, I took out construction loans. They were issued at 75% of the economic value of each home. By doing much of the work myself and bartering for what I couldn't do, I was able to complete the construction with little out-of-pocket expense.

I also had become a bit of a "favorite son" at the local savings and loan. Having a good relationship with the manager in the bank's loan department was helpful in securing my construction loans.

Using a free architectural drafting service (as I'd done with my own home), I designed the houses and had blueprints made. My vision was to build energy-efficient, low-maintenance brick houses on beautifully landscaped lots.

I built the first house, and when it was done, I had an open house.

I put little signs everywhere. The signs said things like:

"Extra Insulation" "Extra Modern Piping"

"Trouble-Free, Maintenance-Free Plumbing" "Maintenance-Free Copper Pipes" "Maintenance-Free Outside Brick"

I was pushing my quality. People were impressed. That first house, and all ten others, sold quickly. Each was sold for between $30,000 and $35,000. These were excellent prices, and they netted me a very nice profit. I was ecstatic with the success of this project: my first housing development.

Like my experience at the fair as a youth—and like my first car-buying experience, when I started with a good used car instead of a brand-new car—this was a lesson in the importance of saving and investing. Rather than spending money on something that wouldn't grow in value, I turned that small investment into something big.

I recommend that anyone who wants to be an entrepreneur, regardless of field, take this approach. Instead of spending money in ways that won't add significant value over time, figure out how you can best make your money work and grow for *you*.

GOOD NEIGHBORS

There was one snag with those eleven homes, and it had nothing to do with the financing or the construction. Those things were no problem. What *was* a problem, I learned, was who got to live in the neighborhood. A couple from the Philippines came to one of my open houses.

It was a husband and wife, both of them impeccably dressed. After they'd looked around, the husband told me, "We love your house, and we want to buy it." Then he said, "Would you please come to our current house in Rock Island and have a cup of tea with us?"

"Certainly," I said. "But why?"

"We want to show you how we live," he said. "We want you to see that we'll take care of the house and be good neighbors to your other buyers."

At that time, most people I knew were either German immigrants like me, or else businessmen, all of them white, most of whom came from families that had been in the United States for a long time. I didn't know many people from other backgrounds. I didn't realize that white Americans could be so discriminatory against Filipinos and other people of color.

"I'll come over this evening," I told the couple.

I went to their home, and they served me a cup of tea. Their house was in a very poor neighborhood, but their home was well kept up, clean, and pristine. They were gracious hosts, and I enjoyed getting to know them. The next day, we drew up the contract for them to buy the house I had for sale.

When the neighbors found out that I'd shown a house to Filipinos and they had a contract to buy it, they were up in arms. I decided to hold a meeting for the other homeowners.

I gave it to them straight. I told them, "You ought to be ashamed of yourselves." I said to one of them, "Joe, you have a restaurant. You serve those people food, and you never ask any questions, do you? How is this different? Now, stop making waves."

The neighbors still weren't happy about it, but they simmered down. The Filipino couple and their family moved in, and—no surprise to me—they turned out to be the nicest neighbors. In time, everybody was proud to have them in the neighborhood.

I could have handled this situation differently. I could have given

in to the pressure and refused to sell the house to the Filipino couple. There were no antidiscrimination laws in those days, so I had no legal obligation to sell to them. I didn't need to worry that they'd sue me if I didn't sell the house to them. We all knew that if I said no, they'd have zero recourse.

Alternatively, I could have sold the house to them but never discussed it with the neighbors and community members. I could have said, "Too bad for you. You can't do anything about it." But I wanted to talk with them and try to convince them of the wisdom in selling to the couple. I wanted people to feel comfortable about this wonderful couple living in the neighborhood.

Reaching out to the community didn't 100% solve the problem, but it did go a long way. I'm sure that if I'd never held that meeting, there would have been much more animosity toward the Filipino homeowners, and toward me. In the long run, I was protecting not only the couple and their family, but my business as well.

In business, as in life, you can never underestimate the importance of communication, and of holding steadfast to your values.

PARADE OF HOMES

I wasn't a bricklayer anymore. I wasn't even a mason contractor anymore. I still had bricklayers working for me, of course. However, now I was a home builder. My company that I founded, which I now called the Paulsen Construction Company, was in the business of building and selling homes.

Around this time, I joined the Quad Cities Home Builders Association. In 1962, they elected me to chair the Quad Cities Parade of Homes committee. For the Parade of Homes, each builder in the association featured a show home that was open to the community to view, inside and out. Of course, we builders put our best foot forward for this event!

Since I was chairman of the committee, I was determined to have the most impressive house that anybody had ever seen. I used one of the lots I'd previously contracted, at 3730 Nineteenth Avenue in Moline, and designed a house for that lot. The floor plan I came up with was, in my mind, efficient and clever. My house was a splitlevel, which was becoming common in that era, but I took things up a notch.

My design included two above-grade levels. On the main floor, there was a living room and kitchen. Five steps up, there were three bedrooms and a bathroom. All of that was fairly standard, but below level, things got really interesting.

Because of how harsh winters are in Illinois, incorporating square footage below the frost line adds to a structure's efficiency. Five steps down from the main level was what the newspapers called an "English-style" basement, with windows at ground level. It had a rec room with a large fireplace and a TV built into the wall. It was open to the back yard, with five steps to the garage. On this level, there was also an office and a second bathroom. Five steps down from this level was a deeper basement, with no windows. It featured a playroom and a bar area that ran the length of one side.

The kitchen had state-of-the-art appliances, including Nutone built-ins. I put in an intercom, so people on each level could communicate without yelling.

The Nineteenth Avenue house had the finest brickwork. There was a stone fireplace in the living room and a brick fireplace in the "English-style" basement. I did the fireplace stonework and brickwork myself, in the evenings. I didn't trust my bricklayers with those fireplaces.

Knowing that I was creating something unique, something that lots of people would want to see, I went to a cabinetry company and said, "Give me the best cabinets you have. You can put your name on them, and people will appreciate your good quality. I'm going to have a lot of showings here, and I'm pushing the quality. The house will be in every magazine. Trust me."

I went to Pella, a window company based in Pella, Iowa, and told them the same thing. "I want the best windows you have. But I want them at a discount, because my home is going to be the most popular house in the Quad Cities Parade of Homes." Pella gave me windows at cost.

Furniture? Same thing. I went to Ethan Allen, the best furniture company in town. I said, "I want your furniture in my house, but I can't pay you for the furniture. You can take it out after the Parade of Homes is over. But during the two weeks the Parade is going on, you can put your sign on the furniture and reap the rewards of people seeing your good-quality furniture in a fantastic setting." They furnished the house to a T. It was amazing.

The day before the Parade of Homes opened, an editorial I wrote was printed in the *Quad-City Times*. Among the things I said was, "People who visit the Parade of Homes will get a chance to look at many new products and ideas. If there are any QuadCitians interested in buying a new home, they will have a good selection in the Parade. Most buyers will benefit in buying a Parade home... Anyone who is interested in buying a home in the near future should look around this fall and start thinking about buying now."

As for my house in the Parade, there was a two-page spread about it in *The Moline Dispatch*. There was such buzz about it, even *Better Homes and Gardens*, out of Chicago, did an article on my house before construction was complete. Another article was titled, "Paulsen Has Showplace."

On weekends during the Parade of Homes, people stood in line for forty-five minutes to go through my house. I had to get police officers to direct traffic. It was incredible.

After the Parade of Homes, I told Elke, "We're not selling this house. It's too beautiful to sell. We're going to have to move into it ourselves." So, we put our first house on the market and moved into the house on Nineteenth Avenue.

By this time, my daughters were five, three, and two. We moved into the house and greatly enjoyed living there.

I also must give Elke credit for helping when I built that house. She supported me by handling our household and even helping some with the business. She'd be at home, and I'd be at the building site, where of course we had no phone. This was long before the days of cellphones. But we did have two-way radios, and the signal reached our home. I'd radio Elke and get her to call in orders for concrete, lumber, and other materials. That was a huge help to me.

My daughter, Susan, says, "In 2014, Dad and I went back to visit Moline to celebrate the birthday of his brother, my Uncle Werner. We went to the house on Nineteenth Avenue, and to our surprise, the lady who answered was—all grown up now, of course—a girl who'd been our babysitter. Her mother lived on the next street over. The woman who now owned the home said that ever since she was a young girl, this was the house she'd wanted to own, and now she did. She gave us a tour. To my astonishment, I really got to see my father's craft, in a way I hadn't noticed as a child, of course. His ability to lay bricks was like that of an artist. The front entry had a brick planter box. The living room and basement family room fireplaces were of stonework that encompassed entire walls. They were rich and beautiful, and they looked exactly as they did when I was a child." Susan goes on, "Afterwards, Dad and I drove around Moline, and as we drove down various streets, he'd point and say, 'I built that one,' and 'I built that one, too.' It was apparent which homes he built, because they were brick all the way around and still looked like new. Of course, the trees were huge after all those decades, but the houses were in great shape and looked beautiful."

I'm proud of the fact that, all these years later, the homes I built in Moline have stood the test of time. Other than the first house I built for Elke and me, these homes were my first forays into building complete structures entirely the way I wanted them built. There were people who advised me to cut corners to save money, but I did things *my* way—and now, almost sixty years later, it's crystal clear that I made the right decisions.

My brother Werner did the same with custom homes as I did. He bid on contract for individual owners. Matter of fact, one of his homes that he built for an individual owner came up for sale later, and the home warranted a high price because in the real estate listing, it said it was a Werner Paulsen home.

Again, if you're going to be in business—any business—you have to consider these factors. Could you cut corners and run your business cheaply? Sure, you could. But in the long run, that will cost you, either in your reputation or in dissatisfied customers wanting to return your product for a refund (not possible with a house, of course, but certainly possible in many other businesses). Cutting corners could even, potentially, cost you because of customers taking legal action against you. To avoid this, your best bet is to provide the highest quality product or service you can, and price whatever you're selling appropriately.

ON THE MAP

The 1962 Parade of Homes really put me on the map. At one time known in Moline as "the German kid," I was now referred to throughout the Quad Cities as, "the Parade of Homes Guy."

I continued to build house after house. Everyone in Moline knew who I was. If they bought a Peter Paulsen home, they knew they were getting the best quality possible.

I always held my own open houses. I didn't want to pay a realty company, and I was worried they wouldn't do as good a job of selling a home as I could. I wanted to be in charge of explaining the value of the home to a potential customer. I had my own open houses on Sundays, and I did all my own selling.

At the time, I also did my own billing and accounting. In those days, you didn't use title companies for real estate transactions. Title companies were just getting started, and they were not required. I just used a law firm, which did the abstract of title. Later, as my business expanded, I hired a private secretary.

I worked with the same philosophy I'd always used. I wasn't interested in building homes for people who wanted the cheapest bid and were willing to settle for low quality. I didn't want to live that way, and I didn't want the people buying the houses I built to live that way, either.

What I realized was that I could make double the money by building my own homes and selling their perceived value. Never mind what it costs; what I was selling was perceived value. I created homes of exceptional quality. I sold them at a good price, and they sold fast. For each project, I'd get a construction loan from the savings and loan company. I paid the lot off, then I had a reserve, which I used to build the house. I sold homes for twice what it cost me to build them.

The math always added up. If I spent 5% more for quality, I could charge 20% more for the house. That's how I was thinking about it, and it worked.

Susan said, "My dad was always very cutting edge and innovative. Obviously, when you're self-employed, the more efficient you are, the more money you make. I think Dad figured out very early on how to delegate without compromising the quality. He absolutely demanded that quality persevere."

CHALLENGE YOURSELF

- What opportunities have come your way that you acted on? How did it work out?

- Conversely, have there been opportunities you didn't act on, that you now regret? You can't change that now, but what can you do to ensure that in the future, you don't let opportunities pass you by?

- How can you make your money work for you? Even if you only have a small amount of seed money, how can you negotiate terms to make that money grow into something fruitful?

- What are your personal and business values? What can you do to ensure that your business always keeps your values at the forefront?

- In what ways can you provide a quality product or service, yet be creative in how you spend your money to do it, thus ensuring both your own profitability and your customers' satisfaction?

CHAPTER 7

THE FINEST QUALITY APARTMENTS
(1962 – 1963)

A DREAM COME TRUE

One night soon after the Parade of Homes, the man who sold me the original eleven lots I developed rang my doorbell. He said, "Peter Paulsen, I have a very important person in my car who would like to speak to you."

"Oh, yeah?" I said. "Bring him in."

It turned out to be one of the board directors from John Deere. His name was Edmond Cook. He was also a member of the Butterworth family, which had longstanding ties with John Deere. In 1892, William Butterworth, Mr. Cook's ancestor, had married a granddaughter of John Deere (the company founder) and joined the business. Mr. Cook was a multimillionaire, the richest man in Moline.

He said, "Mr. Paulsen, you've done work for our friends with fireplaces, and you have a good reputation. I'm the executor of the estate for a large parcel of land near the Butterworth Center, here in town. I'd like to have an apartment complex built on that parcel.

Many directors at John Deere are interested in apartment living. We want luxury, well-appointed apartments. I'm a director of Chicago Steel, too, and I keep an apartment in Chicago to use when I'm there. I'm a director of Weyerhaeuser Lumber Company, and I have an apartment near that company. But there are no deluxe apartment complexes in Moline. John Deere would like you to build one." He went on, "The lot isn't zoned for apartments. Rezoning has been proposed twice, but the neighbors are against it. They use the lot as a baseball diamond. Another developer was turned down by City Hall and couldn't get it done. So, your first step would be to get the rezoning through."

I'd read a lot about rezoning, and I felt I understood the subject well. "I can do that," I said. "How much do you want for the lot?"

"Two hundred thousand," Mr. Cook replied.

I started to laugh. "Jesus," I said. "I don't have that kind of money."

"Don't worry," he told me. "I can sell it to you with no money down and no interest until you get a construction loan. I'm the executor of the estate, I control the lot, and I'd like to live on that property. It has a good view of the ravine and the woods." "Okay," I said. "Mr. Cook, you've got a deal."

By this time, I'd read so many books about apartment buildings—covering issues such as building and financing them, apartment construction, geographical location of apartments, how the population was expanding, and how there was going to be a big need for apartments—that I felt I knew the topic inside out. I still had my dream of developing and owning apartment buildings. In the years during which I'd become a successful builder of single-family homes, that dream had never died.

Do you recall what I said earlier about opportunities? You can't let them slip by. And this was an amazing one. After Mr. Cook left, I said to myself, "Here's my chance, a full twenty years ahead of my expectations."

COMMUNICATION IS KEY

I sketched floor plans for the apartments and my vision for the plot plan. I proposed three buildings, each of them two stories tall, constructed entirely of brick. They would be situated on the lot in a U-shape, with covered parking in the back and a park setting in the middle. The park would be four hundred feet in length and two hundred feet in width. I wanted it to be beautifully landscaped, so people who walked by on the sidewalk would see something appealing when they turned their heads—and people who lived in the apartments would feel like they had their own private park to enjoy. I decided to call the complex Townecrest Manor. I took my sketches to an architecture firm and had them draw up formal plans. I also had a rendering of the apartment complex done. Then, for the next two weeks, I knocked on every door in the neighborhood.

After introducing myself, I said, "I want you to know what I'm building, so you'll be happy with my construction, and you won't object at City Hall." I showed them my plans and rendering, and everyone was impressed. I got to know the neighbors, who were all pleasant people. Turned out they really didn't mind losing their ball field. They just wanted to be sure something beautiful would be on that lot. The developers who made earlier proposals either didn't bother to show the neighbors their plans, or else their plans were unattractive. With any project, communication is key. I think it's important to include people in decisions that affect them. If people feel that you're listening to them and truly want to understand their concerns, they'll be much more willing to work with you.

My methodology worked. I took my plans to City Hall and got 100% approval. Not a single objection.

TOWNECREST MANOR: THE NUMBERS

I studied everything I could about financing apartment buildings. I developed a financial plan of income and expenses. The appraisal for an investment property is based on net income. I knew from the books I'd read that you total what your net income will be, and you multiply it by ten times in earnings. From this, you come up with a value for the property.

My rental rate was very high, three times the average rate of apartments in Moline at the time. As mentioned, appraisal is based on income, rather than construction cost. Because of my high rental rate, the appraisal for Townecrest Manor was also very high.

I knew I'd be able to charge a sizable rent for these apartments, because of their high quality, good location, and great floor plans. Because of this, there would be a high value for the complex and per unit. Being my own contractor, with my own masons and carpenters, I knew I could build the property for 75% of the appraised value.

The value I came up with was $1,000,000. I needed a 75% construction loan, or $750,000.

I created a schematic for the finances and took it to an insurance company, which one of the books said I should do. I went to Prudential Insurance Company and asked for a forward commitment loan. Again, I knew how to do that because of the books I'd read. And I received my commitment from the insurance company.

Then I took my commitment to the bank. I said to the loan officer, "Here's my commitment from the insurance company. I'd like a construction loan from you for the building of the apartments. When the apartment construction is completed, you'll get bought out by the insurance company."

The loan officer said, "How do you know you can get the construction done?"

"Well," I replied. "Ask the John Deere people about me. They know you can trust me."

So the bank checked my references. By this time, I had such a good reputation in the Quad Cities area, all the references were glowing.

Still, the loan officer said, "We want a bond that you can complete it. We also want a life insurance policy on you, in case you die, because we won't get stuck with a building we don't know how to complete."

"Fine," I said. "I'll do all of that."

All of this demonstrates several things. First, research is key. Never would I have taken on a project of that size without doing my homework first. I needed to know what I was talking about, and my numbers had to be solid. If you start a business or take on a huge project without doing the research first, your chances of failure are that much greater.

Second, your reputation is golden. No matter what line of work you're in, make sure you're providing a quality product or service, treating your customers right, and always acting with integrity. If you do that, others will respect you and will recommend you. And that can go a long way toward helping you achieve your goals.

Third, you must be willing to negotiate. The loan officer's requests were reasonable. It was true that if something happened to me before I finished the project, they *would* be stuck with a building they didn't know how to complete. Therefore, I had no problem agreeing to their terms about the bond and the life insurance policy.

TOWNECREST MANOR GOES UP!

Out of the construction loan, I paid for the lot. After that, construction commenced. I had my own bricklayers and my own carpenters. I used aluminum windows because they required zero maintenance. Each unit had insulated window glass, and the buildings were all brick exterior. As I had on previous projects, I used copper plumbing, so I wouldn't end up with corroded pipes.

To have this type of quality construction, I had to charge fairly high rent. My competitors said, "Peter's rent is triple what everybody else is charging for apartments. That's stupid. Peter is out of touch with reality. Nobody's going to pay that kind of rent. Peter's going to fail and go bankrupt."

But they were wrong. Mr. Cook took two apartments on the back side and put in a private elevator and a private garage. I charged him for that, which was no problem. He wanted those amenities, regardless of the cost.

Because Mr. Cook wanted to live in Townecrest Manor, the interest of other executives was piqued. I showed them the layouts, and I had 100% of the units rented before construction was complete.

This isn't to say everything on that project was a breeze. I had numerous disagreements with the local building inspector. More than once, he wanted to shut down construction of Townecrest Manor. Each time that happened, I'd go back to the Uniform Building Code book and check the codes. If I needed clarification, I sent a telegram to the UBC main office in Los Angeles.

One time, the building inspector wanted to shut down my project and said the only way to resolve the dispute was to take it to City Hall. But a meeting wasn't on the schedule for another thirty days. I said, "I can't shut down my project for thirty days. I need a meeting tomorrow." I was so persistent I got my meeting the next day. We resolved the issue, and construction of Townecrest Manor continued.

I got to know those building codes so well, eventually I was named chairman of the local Uniform Building Code committee.

As for Townecrest Manor, numerous John Deere executives moved in. John Deere had executives from around the world come to Moline, and most of them didn't want to buy a house. They needed temporary but high-quality housing.

Marketing the apartments was easy. They rented fast because I had the high-end market all to myself. A lot of retired lawyers, judges, and executives, as well as high-end businesspeople, rented in Townecrest Manor. All of them were people who wanted a nice place to live but didn't want the hassle of owning a house.

That said, one of the big selling points of Townecrest Manor was that the floor plans were more like those of a house than of a typical apartment. Some units were multistoried, with two bedrooms upstairs, a living room, kitchen, and dining room on the main level, and even a basement that people could turn into a rec room. The master bedrooms were large enough for a king-sized bed. The units had plenty of room for a dining room set and a living room set. Each one had a kitchen with a breakfast area. They ranged in size from 1,100 to 1,500 square feet, and every inch was good, livable space.

Townecrest Manor was an instant success. The first residents took occupancy in November 1962. My floor plans were featured in magazines and newspapers. It was the only luxury apartment complex in Moline at the time, and it was very popular.

In those years, I didn't realize I was actually creating a retirement community. There were no children living in the complex. People with kids couldn't afford to live there, and besides, most people with kids prefer living in a house with a yard. Townecrest Manor appealed to people aged 50 and over who wanted to live in a quiet, beautiful, hassle-free community.

FRIENDS AND MENTORS

During those years when I was building my business, Elke and I still primarily socialized with other Germans, both friends and family. But as generally happens when you have young children, we also got to know other people with kids the same age as our daughters. They were all nice people, but many of them were goofing off while I was working. I couldn't relate to them. As a result, instead of befriending these guys who were my age, I became friends with some of their dads. From a business perspective, I had much more in common with middle-aged men than I did with men my own age.

My new friends, these middle-aged businessmen, were all professionals: lawyers, doctors, and the like. They were impressed with me because I was so young. Their kids were the same age as me. But their kids were on the beach playing volleyball while I was running my business.

As it turned out, my mentor in business, the man I looked up to the most, was Edmond Cook, the man who'd sold me the lot on which I built

Townecrest Manor.

Mr. Cook could tell I was interested in business. At the time, John Deere was building a new headquarters in the hills on the outskirts of Moline. It was to be built of Cor-Ten steel on the outside. Cor-Ten is a type of weathered steel that looks like it's rusted, but it never actually rusts. It never needs painting, so it's very durable and maintenance-free.

Mr. Cook took me to his office and showed me the plans for the new headquarters. Another day, he showed me the plan for a site in Tacoma, Washington, where they were building the new Weyerhaeuser Lumber Company headquarters. That one also used the same technology and the same kind of steel.

Over the years, Mr. Cook shared a great deal with me. He'd ask my opinion about John Deere products. He asked what I thought of the riding lawnmower, which was a product they were developing at that time. He was interested in me personally, in my thinking as an everyday working man rather than an executive.

None of my other friends knew Mr. Cook. Some of them knew *of* him, but my close friends—my German friends—were not friends with him, because he was way out of their financial league.

Looking back at that experience now, I think Mr. Cook spent so much time with me because it was gratifying for him to share his passion, thoughts, and knowledge about construction and business with someone who was interested. We all need someone to listen to us, and I was the one who was eager to listen to him.

This is why the mentor-mentee relationship is rewarding for both parties. The mentee, certainly, has the opportunity to learn a lot. But the mentor is rewarded, too, by having someone to talk with who is genuinely interested in the same subjects.

ON THE MISSISSIPPI

One time, Mr. Cook said to me, "Peter, would you like to see my boat on the Mississippi River?"

"Sure, I would," I replied.

We went one morning around ten o'clock. It was about a 45-minute drive. Mr. Cook's river barge was located in the Mississippi River marina, next to a landing platform.

I was so impressed. I'd never seen anything like that in my life. Mr. Cook's river barge was about sixty feet long. It had two staterooms. It had a bathroom with a shower and marble tiles.

I liked the way the barge was just floating on the Mississippi River. It was docked at the marina on the river; we didn't go out cruising.

Mr. Cook told me, "My wife and I cruise on the weekends, and we take longer trips during the summer. Everybody thinks we're crazy, just cruising, but we love going up and down the Mississippi."

"I don't think you're crazy," I said. "I think it sounds like a damn good idea."

On the way home, he said, "I'm hungry. You want to stop for a hamburger?"

We stopped at a burger joint, and when the bill came, I said, "Mr. Cook, I'm going to pay for this one, because I owe it to you. You showed me a beautiful day today."

Mr. Cook was a multimillionaire. He certainly could have picked up the tab, and I'm sure he would have offered if I didn't do so first. But he was impressed that I paid for our lunch that day. That was the first time in my life I bought lunch for a millionaire. I've done that many times since, and for billionaires, too.

Why would I do that? Why not keep my money in my pocket, when I know the other person would have no problem footing the bill?

The reason goes back to relationships. Building relationships is a vital factor of success in any field. To build relationships, you have to see everyone as a person, as an individual. It didn't matter that Mr. Cook was wealthy; it was proper for me to pay.

Everyone, no matter how much money they have, is a human being. We all like feeling special, and one way to make people feel special is to spend a little money on them. It shows them that you care. Even people who have plenty of money appreciate knowing that other people care about them—as a person.

On the way home, I thought, *someday I'm going to have my own boat, too.*

A LITTLE MORE PRESTIGE

Once Townecrest Manor was built, I said to myself, "That went so well, I have such a waiting list for more units, I'm going to build another complex." But this time, I decided, I'd make it a little bigger, a little better, and with a little more prestige.

I located a lot for my new complex on Forty-fourth Street in Moline. I decided to call the complex Paulsen Manor. Again, I sketched floor plans and a plot plan. They were excellent floor plans. I included one-, two and three-bedroom apartments in my plans, ranging from about 700 to 1,700 square feet. Each unit would have a vestibule, many with walk-in coat closets. The living rooms ranged from sixteen by eighteen feet to twenty-five by fourteen feet. Next to the living room, I added a dining area, none smaller than nine by eleven feet. Everything was generously sized, allowing people to bring their own furniture and not worry about whether it would fit. There would be a utility room, complete with washer and dryer, in every unit. Most units had one bathroom, but deluxe three-bedroom units had two bathrooms. (In those days, people didn't expect as many bathrooms as they do now.) The walls would be heavily insulated, using double wall construction for soundproofing, so that neighbors wouldn't disturb one another.

The plot plan included a swimming pool, which no other apartment complex in Moline had at the time, as well as a recreation building, complete with kitchen and pool table, located away from the main living spaces of the complex. I got that idea out of the books, too a place for residents to gather and to reserve for their own private parties.

"I AM THE DAD."

Word quickly got out that I was building another complex. On December 6, 1962, *The Moline Dispatch* ran a front-page story with the headline, "Paulsen to Build 58 Units." It explained the nine building project and gave the building site's address, which was on Forty-first Street.

By noon, my phone started ringing. One man said, "Mr. Paulsen, I see you have a new apartment complex going up. Our friends live in your other complex, the Townecrest Manor, and are very pleased and happy there. We want to rent from you. Can I see the new complex?" "There's nothing to see," I told him. "I just have stakes in the ground."

"I want to see it anyway," he said.

"All right," I replied. "I'll meet you there at two o'clock."

At two o'clock, I arrived at the job site in my pickup truck. I was 28 years old, but I was skinny from all the labor I did. I looked like I was 16.

When the man arrived, I said, "I'm Peter Paulsen. You called to see the complex."

"Yeah," he replied. "But I talked to your dad this morning. I'll wait until he gets here."

I smiled and said, "Thanks but I *am* the dad."

HIGH-END CONSTRUCTION

There was great anticipation about Paulsen Manor. One man told me, "You have no idea, Peter, how pleased we are that you're building this. We've been trying to get my mother into an apartment for the last five years, and she won't move. But she'll move now. She told us, 'At Paulsen Manor, I can keep my own furniture and dining room set that I've curated and loved so dearly. The only way I'm moving is into a Paulsen apartment.'"

Paulsen Manor was an instant success. By the time it was completed, all the units were rented, just like at my first apartment complex. At one point, some years later, Elke and I lived in Paulsen Manor with our daughters. *The Quad-City Times* did a two-page spread on our apartment, showcasing the layout as well as our furniture and décor. When you look at the pictures in this article (including one of Elke sitting in the living room), you'd never believe you were looking at an apartment. The rooms are so spacious, it looks like a house.

In September 1964, *American Builder* magazine ran a story about apartment-complex development. I was quoted several times. One of the points I made was this one: "'Let your first residents help sell the rest of your project.' Says Moline, Ill. builder Peter Paulsen, 'Our best salesmen are the people who live here. We encourage prospects to talk to local residents and ask them how they like Paulsen Manor. Before we know it, they've sold themselves.'"

To this day, that complex is still called Paulsen Manor Apartments. I don't own it anymore—I sold it decades ago—but it still has my name on it, and they still have a waiting list of five or six years down the road. The only vacancy occurs when somebody dies.

One reason there was absolutely no turnover or vacancy until someone died was because the carpeting and draperies weren't included. I required the tenants to select and pay for their own carpeting and draperies. I learned about this from visiting upscale apartments in downtown Chicago, where carpeting and draperies were never included. My tenants loved the idea; customizing their unit gave them pride. It wasn't unusual for the ladies living in Paulsen Manor to invite other residents over for coffee and to show off their selections. During those times, I frequently had lunch with my banker friends. They liked taking me out to lunch, just to see what I was up to next. I enjoyed spending time with them, and I still miss them. They were all around twenty years older than me, so they've all passed away, of course.

The bankers had followed my progress on Townecrest Manor, and as the Paulsen Manor project continued, they were quite interested. One of them ended up moving into a unit in Paulsen Manor and he lived there until he died.

Again, I created a retirement community.

CAN'T QUIT NOW

I think I was so successful building apartment complexes and single family homes in Moline because I had an innate sense of what people wanted. Whether it was a house with a yard or an apartment in a large complex with lots of amenities, everything was of the best quality, with the most thoughtful layouts and features.

Being successful at what I'd set out to do—develop and sell homes, and then develop and own apartment complexes—gave me a huge sense of accomplishment. But at the same time, I was also building a future. I was thinking about creating sufficient wealth that someday, I wouldn't have to work. Once those two apartment complexes were built, rented, and remained at 100% occupancy, I'd achieved that.

The irony? I realized that no matter how much money I had, I didn't want to retire. The last thing I wanted to do, when I wasn't even 30 years old yet, was quit working.

I loved what I was doing; I couldn't imagine quitting. I just had to figure out what came next.

CHALLENGE YOURSELF

• If you've ever been faced with an enormous opportunity that also posed some risks, did you take the opportunity or turn it down? Why did you make the choice you did?

• Assess your communication skills. Even if you're introverted, communicating with others and getting your ideas across is key to business success. Think about how you communicate best, whether that's with written words, spoken words, or in some other way. How can you play up your communication skills to help build your success?

• Do you like doing research? If not, what steps could you take to make research more interesting for you? Remember that research and careful planning are also key to business success!

• Do you have a mentor? Have you ever mentored someone else? If not, how could you go about finding mentoring opportunities, as a mentee and/or a mentor?

• What is your biggest accomplishment? How can you build on that success to move on to further achievements?

CHAPTER 8
CALIFORNIA, HERE I COME
(1965 – 1977)

LAND OF OPPORTUNITY

Like many American families, my wife, kids, and I watched a lot of television during the 1950s and 1960s. In those years, I was a huge fan of *Davy Crockett*, as portrayed by Fess Parker.

Later, we all also loved Parker in *Daniel Boone*, which aired from 1964 - 1970.

Another of our favorite shows was *The Beverly Hillbillies*, which was on the air from 1962 until 1971. If you don't remember this show, it was about the Clampetts, a family from the Ozarks, who strike oil on their land. When that happens, they decide to move to Beverly Hills, California. The show hilariously contrasts the humble, down-home Clampetts with the wealthy Californians. The main character, Jed Clampett, was played by Buddy Ebsen, who had also starred in *Davy Crockett*.

We loved *The Beverley Hillbillies* and other shows that took place in California. At that time, probably in large part due to Hollywood and the TV studios, people from all over the country were drawn to California. Suddenly, California seemed like *the* place to be. The weather, of course, was beautiful. Reportedly, jobs were numerous and paid well. Just like the gold prospectors of a century earlier, people were flocking to the West Coast in search of their fortunes.

I did some research to find out if the hype was true. Based on what I learned, it did seem to me that California provided plenty of opportunity to build one's wealth and success.

It was 1963, and I was 29 years old. I told Elke, "This is good. We have three kids; we don't need any more. I've done what I set out to do. We have enough money to live the rest of our lives comfortably. We could retire now, but I don't want to retire. Instead, let's think about moving to California, where I can look for real estate investment and development opportunities."

For a year, we didn't do anything except talk about it and make plans. I decided to get a realtor's license before we moved to California. I figured that if I didn't pass the California real estate exam, then I didn't know enough for us to relocate, and we wouldn't go. Using a mail order course, I studied the license requirements for California realtors on the weekends and in the evenings.

I sent in my test and I passed! I said to Elke, "Okay, now we're free to go to California. I can get a real estate license there, which connects me with the real estate world again, without having to fall off the deep end by making a mistake out there."

I figured that having a realtor's license would help me get a foot in the door with California real estate companies. Instead of the "black gold" (i.e., oil) that Jed Clampett discovered on his land, my gold would come in the form of using my new real estate license, combined with my experience developing apartment complexes and single-family homes, to further grow my business. But I'd do it on the West Coast, rather than in Moline, Illinois.

As an aside, years later I became friends with Fess Parker. I was invited to his sixtieth birthday party, and who should be sitting at my table but Buddy Ebsen. I'd never imagined that I would meet somebody like that!

DON'T LEAVE, PAULSENS

In Moline, people didn't want us to leave. The vice chairman of John Deere, Edmond Cook, wrote me a four-page letter about why I shouldn't leave Moline and go to California. That man, as well as my banker friends and other Moline businesspeople, wanted me to stay in Moline because I was a young businessman who could help the town thrive and grow. And, as mentioned earlier, I was also serving as chairman of the Home Builders Association, as well as chairman of the local Uniform Building Code committee.

But Elke was on board with the move, and so were our daughters. We all wanted to try something new, so in October 1964, we packed up and left. We bought a three-bedroom house in Los Altos, which is not far from San Jose.

My goal was to build apartment complexes, just as I'd done in Moline. I immediately joined the Apartment Owners Association to study what other people were doing in apartments. I joined real estate associations and the Chamber of Commerce. I went to every meeting I could. I wanted to get connected quickly and establish myself in the community.

I also wanted to get a foot in the door with California real estate companies. Using the real estate license I'd acquired, I worked as a realtor for a commercial real estate firm. I wasn't wild about working for someone else, but it was a good way to get started in a new community and to learn about the "other side" of the real estate world, the one in which I hadn't yet spent much time, as my previous work was in residential real estate. I learned a lot, and I met quite a few people.

This is a lesson in being flexible. Was selling and renting commercial real estate, working for someone else, my dream job? Not at all. But was it a means to an end, a way to get to know people and to better understand the community? Absolutely, it was.

It's important not to let your mental picture of the perfect job or the perfect situation get in the way of an experience that can be a stepping-stone. You don't have to do it forever. But you *do* have to show up every day with a smile on your face, ready to work, to learn, and to help other people. By doing that, you'll make the most of your time, even in a job that's not your "dream job."

BACK TO MOLINE

Elke, our kids, and I all enjoyed living in Los Altos. That said, a year after we moved to California, we decided to move back to Moline. We were homesick for our friends in the Midwest, and we remembered only the good parts. We kept thinking about barbecues and picnics with friends and family. I still owned Townecrest Manor and Paulsen Manor, and I had been long-distance working on plans for expanding Paulsen Manor.

When we moved back in September 1965, we settled in one of the largest units in Paulsen Manor. We even got a mention in *The Moline Dispatch*, in a story about Quad-City comings and goings: "All the folks out there [in Paulsen Manor] rejoiced when Peter Paulsen, his wife and children returned after living in California a short time." And, as I mentioned in the last chapter, *The Quad-City Times* did a two-page spread about our beautiful, spacious apartment in Paulsen Manor.

At this time, I began to develop several other apartment buildings around town. A few months later, I was named chairman for the 1966 Parade of Homes.

From a business perspective, all was well. I was successful in Moline, as I'd always been. And we were happy to be back with our family and friends.

Around this time, the John Deere board members and the local bankers called me into a meeting. They said, "Peter, downtown Moline needs redevelopment, and we've created a committee to get that done. Our committee would like to give you carte blanche to develop downtown as you see fit. Whatever you want to do with it, it's open for you to do."

Of course, it wasn't *really* carte blanche. Everything would still have to go through their committee and the officials at City Hall.

I thanked them but said, "The reality is, I'd be working with somebody else. I'd be at someone else's whims. I can't function that way. I'm too fast moving. I make a decision in a split second, but everybody would want a ten-page report and the chance to 'think about it' for a month. I can't work like that that." So I turned down their offer.

Then summer rolled around. We'd forgotten about the 90% humidity in the Midwest. We ended up spending a lot of time indoors, where there was air conditioning. And we knew winter would arrive again, with its snow and freezing temperatures. We longed for the mild California climate we'd come to love.

My daughter, Susan, shares this recollection: "Some years ago, during the time when Dad and I went back to Moline for the ninety-fifth birthday of Tanta Tieda, Dad's aunt, it was a crisp, beautiful day, but it was seventeen degrees out. After years of living in California, I felt like I was in a meat locker!" Susan goes on, "Looking back, when we moved the second time, I think it was because my dad realized that building in the Midwest was so much more limiting. The winter cold and the summer heat and humidity made development challenging. In California, anything could happen year-round—and it could happen quickly, which was exactly my dad's style."

Susan is absolutely right. Despite the fact that we had no extended family in California, both personal and professional factors played into the decision to move there a second time.

The long and short of it is, we learned that you can't have absolutely everything. We couldn't have our close friends and family nearby *and* live in a beautiful, up-and-coming place like California. We had to choose, and we decided to give California another try. We knew we could always come back and visit Moline anytime.

So, eighteen months later, in early 1967, we moved back out west.

A CUSTOM-BUILT HOUSE

The second time we moved to California, we settled in the town of Saratoga, about fifteen miles southwest of San Jose. I built my family a beautiful, custom-designed two-story house on Lenark Lane.

Susan says, "When the Lenark Lane house was under construction, Dad would get us kids to clean up the construction site every night. Hey, why not? It was free child labor." She continues, "One time, Veronica fell through the upstairs and landed on the concrete entry foyer floor. She was okay, could still walk, but Dad did take her to the doctor—that time, anyway."

I was practical. I knew I could fix that knee myself, so why should I pay for a doctor?

Susan was the "boy" of our family, more like a son to me than my other two daughters were. As my mother had during my childhood, I delegated a lot of responsibility to Susan. I taught her the German work ethic I'd been raised with. I'd say to her, "You're going to do it right. This is not right. It has to be exactly done correctly, or it is not acceptable."

My daughter was a good student, and she always strove for excellence. I think she wanted to please me.

The Saratoga house had windows that were two stories high. Susan was required to hang out the window and use vinegar water to clean both the inside and outside of the double-paned windows. She did a good job; they were immaculate when she was finished. Susan says, "Now, I'm teaching my own grandchildren how to do that. They're little, eight and six, and they don't like doing it, but when they get older, they're going to be great at it, and they'll probably have clean windows."

Susan is correct. If these traditions aren't taught, they die out.

They never get passed on.

GRACIOUS, ELEGANT LIVING

As I had the first time we lived in California, I immediately joined organizations and got to know people. But instead of working for someone else, at this point I incorporated a company called Paulsen Homes, Inc.

One of my first projects was a housing development in the Almaden Country Club area of San Jose. I built three model homes, ranging in size from 2,400 to 2,700 square feet. These were spacious homes with three to four bedrooms and two and a half bathrooms. They were designed for families who wanted a luxury, well-sized, and well-equipped home in a beautiful, up-and-coming area. All the homes in the development sold quickly and the project was very successful.

Unfortunately, not every project went as planned. In Saratoga, the town where we lived, I wanted to develop an apartment complex. I planned to do what I'd done in Moline: build an attractive, luxury apartment complex for semi-retired and retired people who no longer wanted the upkeep of a single-family home. But the area where I wanted to build it was zoned only for single-family homes. Even though I tried to talk with them and share my plans, as I'd done in Moline, the nearby residents protested. As a result, I couldn't get the zoning through for that one.

That was a disappointment, but I'm telling you this story as a reminder that just because one thing doesn't work out, that's never a reason to give up completely. I simply put it aside and concentrated on my next project.

There was a large lot for sale in San Jose, with frontage to the freeway and in a good neighborhood. It was zoned residential for apartments, but not commercial. I put in a bid to buy it and so did another developer. We were bidding back and forth, but I wanted that lot, and I was determined to get it.

Eventually, I won the bid. I put together plans for a 160-unit apartment complex. It would be three stories tall, Spanish-Mediterranean style, with recreational facilities including a pool in the center of the complex, underground parking below the buildings, and overnight guest rooms that tenants' visitors could use.

As I'd done with previous projects, I designed the plot plan and unit layouts myself. For the two-bedroom units, I put the living room in the middle and a bedroom on each side, each with its own private bathroom. When you walked in the front door, the kitchen, dining area, and living room were in front of you, and the bedroom suites were on either side. It was ideal for two roommates to share, each of them allotted plenty of privacy.

I called the complex Villa del Prado. It's on Moorpark Avenue, and these days, it's called The Monterey.

Villa del Prado was completed in 1970. The June 1970 *Homebuilding Apartment's Report* did a five-page spread on the complex, featuring a full-color photo of the complex on the cover of the report, several photos of the units and the grounds, and floor plans of the various apartment layouts. I was quoted in the article thus: "We have designed this apartment with the tenant in mind. In today's competitive market, you have to design apartments at least five years ahead of the times, and this is exactly what we do with all our projects, and as a result, our tenants stay longer."

Villa del Prado was beautiful, but as work was being completed on it, I noticed how many other apartment complexes were going up in the same area. As I mentioned earlier, people were flocking to California in search of great weather and good jobs. Santa Clara County was booming. The name "Silicon Valley" hadn't come into vogue yet, but there were numerous technology companies and other businesses cropping up in the area.

That said, as far as apartments went, the whole region was becoming extensively overbuilt. The apartment supply had begun to exceed demand. I said to myself, "If I can't rent these, I'll have to make a mortgage payment." Besides, even if I could keep my development 100% occupied, apartments meant dealing with broken dishwashers, stopped-up plumbing, and all sorts of other issues.

So, I decided to sell Villa del Prado before I got in trouble financially. I sold it to a group of Salt Lake City investors. I received only a modest profit, but that was much better than getting burned by having the wrong project on my hands. And it gave me enough money to move on to another project.

This is a lesson in being aware of what's going on around you and in trusting your gut. My gut feeling was that it was time to sell that project. I trusted my gut because I could see the writing on the wall. All I had to do was drive around, seeing all those other apartment complexes, and I knew it was best to get out of that business.

But what should come next? I decided apartment complexes were not the way to go.

Instead, I considered the fact that all the people living in the apartments had to work somewhere. That made me wonder: where were their jobs? Where were they working now? And where would they be working as the San Jose area grew?

Because of all the technology in the area, the answer, for many of them, was in offices.

Maybe, I decided, with the growing demand for office space, commercial property development was the way to go. COMMERCIAL DEVELOPMENT

I started my foray into commercial real estate development with one lot, previously occupied by a single-family home. It was in the town of Campbell, which borders San Jose. The lot was on a busy street, just two blocks from a freeway exit. I paid the owner twice what it was worth, tore down the house, and built an 8,000-square-foot commercial building, which rented up instantly.

In that building, I also opened a real estate office. It was staffed with a manager, five realtors, and a secretary. The manager ran the real estate arm of my business, which dealt in commercial, residential, and industrial sales.

As for me, I continued to focus my interests on commercial development. After the success of the Campbell property, I scouted locations and settled on one that was less than a mile from Villa del Prado. Four houses faced Moorpark Avenue, which is the frontage road for the freeway. Behind them, five other houses faced another street, Blackford Avenue. Again, these houses were potential teardowns. Being on the frontage road, the four lots in front were unfavorable to single-family living, but they were perfect for an office complex. The five lots in the back were on a residential street but not far from the frontage road and the highway noise. Each lot was one acre, so if I got them all, I'd have a nine-acre parcel of land.

I went to each homeowner and said, "I want to buy your house. I'll give you almost double what you'd get if you listed it for sale." I bought the houses one at a time, because I didn't have enough money to buy them all at once. After I bought each one, I went to City Hall to get that lot zoned for commercial development.

First, I got zoning approved for the four lots on Moorpark. Then I bought the five houses that faced Blackford, and I got zoning approval for commercial development for those lots, too.

For financing, I used the same principle I'd used in Moline. I went to the bank and got a construction loan and a takeout loan. That allowed me to build everything without any of my own money in it, except for my initial investment in the land. I negotiated 100% financing (i.e., 75% loan to appraisal value), with the idea to develop the buildings one at a time.

I had a friend who was a builder and knew the area well. He said, "Peter, you're never going to get decent commercial rent on Blackford. That's a residential street."

"This is my plan," I told him. "I'm not going to have people enter the complex from Blackford. I'm going to feed them all off Moorpark, with a parking lot in the middle and the buildings around the perimeter. The whole complex will have only one address, on Moorpark Avenue. I'm calling it Paulsen Office Park."

I designed and built Paulsen Office Park with small tenants in mind. Typically, one large, open space was used by a receptionist and several office workers. Then there was a private office on each side of that middle space. The idea was that people didn't have to make up their minds right away what they were going to do with the space. I'd tell potential tenants, "This unit has two private office spaces, a reception area in the middle, and room for two more secretaries or other workers in the middle space. You can share this setup with another businessperson or use it to grow your own business."

I built Paulsen Office Park in the mid-1970s. The final project, when complete, was nine acres and 200,000 square feet of office space. It took several years to fully develop the project. But it turned out to be an instant success. It rented really fast—bingo, bingo, bingo. Each building was 50% rented either before or during construction, and 100% rented within a year of completion.

Each time a building in the complex was completed, about 15%-20% of the tenants for the new building were existing Paulsen Office Park tenants who needed more space. Because my tenants were so satisfied, they wanted to stay in the complex and simply move to a larger space.

Paulsen Office Park was featured in a 1977 publication called *Profit Planning For Real Estate Development: The Complete Guide For Builders, Lenders, and Other Investors*. The feature was titled "Design excellence provides marketing edge." In it, my tenants were described thus: "This entire market is prestige-oriented, and interested in planning with a high degree of environmental character...and they're willing to pay for a superior, well maintained environment. The typical tenant is concept-oriented, as opposed to those who are economic-necessity oriented."

That explains my customer base in a nutshell. The same quality standards I'd brought to single-family homes and apartment complexes, I also brought to my commercial properties.

I was very satisfied with those commercial developments. They fulfilled a need in the community, they were aesthetically pleasing, and they were lucrative for me. Again, doing my research, paying attention to the community's needs, and communicating effectively with other people, were all key to my success.

Looking back, I'm very glad we gave California a second try. Returning to Moline for a year was the right thing to do, because I had some unfinished business there, and because we truly wanted to be sure that California was the right place for us. The year back in Moline gave us a fresh perspective on the two different lifestyles—the Midwest and California—and the second time we went, it was for keeps. Elke passed away in 2021, but she lived the rest of her life in Saratoga, California. Veronica and Lisa also are lifelong Californians. Susan has had several stints in other places, but she's lived most of her life in California.

As for me? Well—to find out where I went and what I did next, read on.

CHALLENGE YOURSELF

• Have you ever made a cross-country move? Would you consider doing so if the right opportunity came your way?

• What training or courses have you taken that could help you realize your dreams?

• Have you ever taken a "stepping-stone" job? How did it work out?

• Do you generally trust your own instincts? If not, what changes could you make that would help you better use your intuition?

• If you're interested in real estate, do your interests lie more with residential or commercial work? What makes you choose this path over the other? (Remember that both are valid paths. It's a matter of choosing what's right for you, and for your present and future circumstances.)

CHAPTER 9
CALIFORNIA CAPIT AL CITY
(1977 – 1984)

ON A PERSONAL NOTE

In the late 1970s, Elke and I divorced. It had been a long time coming, actually. Our lives had taken different directions. She was a good wife and mother, and she cared well for our children.

But I was very busy building my business, and I wasn't around much. Aside from the times we spent boating (more on that later), I was at work much more than I was with my family.

I was, in short, a workaholic. And while I remained devoted to our daughters, I can admit now that I didn't make much time for Elke's and my relationship. Like many couples, we simply grew apart.

Soon afterward, I met a woman named Angela. We got married in 1979 in Hillsborough, California. Our wedding was held at the private residence of Tom Clausen, the president of Bank of America at the time.

Shortly after Angela and I married, I purchased a three-acre lot in Hillsborough, on Santa Inez Avenue, the most expensive street in that town. The parcel was zoned for three homes, but I planned to build only one home on it. I wanted to build an estate—and I did. The house was 14,000 square feet, with a full basement carrying another 7,000 square feet, including a wine cellar and recreation room. During the home's construction, I expected that once I moved in, I'd live there for the rest of my life.

The home took three years to build. Around the time it was completed, but before we moved in, Angela and I took a trip to Santa Barbara. While we were there, we noticed an open house for a home in Montecito, a small community in Santa Barbara County. The home was listed by a realtor named Paul O'Keeffe, who later became a lifelong friend. We toured the house and fell in love with it. We ended up purchasing it before going home. Upon our return to Hillsborough, we put the estate we'd just completed on the market.

The house sold quickly. While it was in escrow, but the sale hadn't yet closed, I received a call from a realtor telling me that Joe Montana, the quarterback for the San Francisco Forty-Niners, was interested in buying it.

"It's already sold," I told the realtor.

He asked me if Montana and his wife could just look at the house, with me present. I agreed and flew up to Hillsborough.

We toured every room of that 21,000-square-foot home. It was obvious how much they loved the house. In each room, Joe Montana's wife leaned over and gave him a kiss on the cheek.

Of course, there was nothing to be done since the house was already in escrow with another buyer. In hindsight, I wonder if Montana would have paid another half million dollars for the house, which I could have given to the original buyer to break off the deal. But I didn't do that, so the original buyer closed on and moved into the house. That house, at 350 Santa Inez Avenue, is now valued at $30 million.

My daughters were growing up and beginning their adult lives. Susan began her college career in San Diego, but eventually moved back to northern California, settling in Paradise and going to school at Chico State University. Veronica needed extra care, and she moved with Angela and me, living in a guest house on our property. Lisa remained in Saratoga with Elke.

ON TO THE NEXT CITY

I loved living in Montecito, but it was small, with few businesses. It wasn't a great area for commercial development. My San Jose properties were completed, fully rented, and easily managed by the employees of my corporation, now called the Peter Paulsen Company. I built an office complex in Newport Beach, California which, like my San Jose properties, was very successful. But it was a one-time project; I knew I didn't want to work extensively in Orange County. All this meant that for me, it was again time for something new.

I had some friends in Sacramento, the capital city of California. Sacramento is the political center of the state, and at that time, businesses of all kinds were cropping up there. The area was booming, and I determined that it was ripe for office building development.

As always, I worked on my own. I was still young, in my midforties, and I had my whole future in front of me. I didn't want anybody else involved, because then I'd have to split the profit and split the decision-making. If you have a partner who thinks differently than you do and tries to dissuade you from doing what you want to do, it can wreak havoc with your future. I know that for some people, a business partnership works. But for me, personally, it's hard to imagine a business partner who would be truly on the same page as me and has the same caliber of entrepreneurship. I wouldn't have considered myself a true entrepreneur if I'd been partnered up with someone else.

I was, and am, so focused. When I have a new project, I eat it, sleep it, and drink it. I put every bit of energy into that project until it's done. It's much easier to do that on your own than with a partner who may or may not have that same level of commitment. For me, that just sounds like an exercise in frustration.

Because I've always focused on one project at a time, I always kept my business to a size where I could pay attention to every detail of what was going on. When I was developing a new project, I didn't want to delegate anything. When a project was completed and was running smoothly—like my office parks in San Jose and Newport Beach, Paulsen Manor back in Moline, and the other developments I still owned—I had property managers and other employees who took care of the day-to-day business of dealing with tenants and maintaining the property. For new projects, however, it was all on me.

In Sacramento, I studied the market, then bought one building lot using the same principles I'd used in San Jose. I built a two-story, 40,000-square-foot office building on that site.

Once that project was completed, I had to figure out what to do next. So again, I studied the market. Next to the Red Lion Hotel in Sacramento, there was a five-acre lot available. The Red Lion was going to buy that land for an expansion, and I decided I better outbid the Red Lion. I went to the shares office of the landholder and made my offer, which was accepted. On that plot of land, I built a five-story, 170,000-square-foot office building called Point West Commerce Center.

Eventually, among the various projects I developed there, I owned over 200,000 square feet of office space in Sacramento.

By then, developing such projects was easy for me. I knew the ins and outs of the business, how to design an attractive, functional space, and how to hire the right contractors to get the job done for a good price and on time.

I also knew everything there was to know about that market. Because of this, my properties rented quickly, and I retained tenants. In a March 1979 article in the *Sacramento Bee*, one of my tenants talks about moving his company (which, during an 18-month period, expanded from two employees to sixteen) from my first office development in Sacramento into Point West. He says, "We were not willing to give up the luxuries and special amenities offered at Paulsen Office Park, so when we outgrew our previous office space, we waited for the new Paulsen building to be completed."

That tenant's experience was typical for Paulsen commercial tenants. I had studied the market and knew exactly what would appeal to tenants and motivate them to pay a premium rent. It's all about knowing your market and your business inside out, and making sure you're meeting a true need in the community.

Because I still enjoyed living in Montecito, and Angela was happy there, too, I didn't even consider moving to Sacramento. It was an easy commute by airplane, so I jetted to Sacramento every week or two. This is something that 17-year-old German immigrant taking his first flight from New York to Chicago in 1952 could never have imagined!

Everything I did was all on my own. I worked, of course, with the banks. The banks were very pleased with how successful my developments were, and they were happy to loan me money. They were waiting in line to front my next project.

Again, I'd learned by now how vital it is to nurture relationships and maintain my reputation. Nothing can take the place of that. If you want to be an entrepreneur of any kind, you *have* to build a reputation in your community. You do that by getting to know people and building trust.

Sacramento taught me, once again, that establishing yourself and building new relationships can be done, even when you move (or move your business) to a different city. It's a matter of taking the time and paying attention to other people.

AN EYE FOR LOCATION

For me, it's always been about location, location, location. As the saying goes, in real estate, those are the three most important things you should be looking for. This is true whether you're in Sacramento or anywhere else in the United States. Location is what you always want to evaluate first.

I've always had a good instinct for locations. That said, I've never simply looked at a plot of land and said, "This is good." In my view, you've got to spend weeks researching a location. You study traffic flow. You see what other new businesses and developments are cropping up nearby. You think about how the public might enter and exit the location. You consider nearby residential areas and try to anticipate public reactions regarding the proposed project. I also put myself in the shoes of tenants. How might the proposed space be used by tenants? In San Jose, I'd specialized in the small office user. I found that in Sacramento, there was the same need for small, flexible office spaces.

Bigger development firms often pay some consultant to give them traffic flow reports on land they're interested in developing. I never paid anyone for that. I'd just drive through the neighborhood, spending a week or so scoping it out. I'd check into a hotel nearby (with Point West, I checked into that Red Lion) and watch what people were doing, where they were going to work. I'd think about whether, and how, my project might fit into the community's needs.

A lot of it is gut feeling. I developed a gut feeling for location, projects, and potential rent. In Sacramento, as I'd done in San Jose, I joined the Builders Association, apartment associations, the Chamber of Commerce, and other groups. I wanted to rub elbows with other developers and businesspeople to learn what they were doing and learn about the city's needs.

I recall one instance when a friend of mine wanted to develop a small office building in Fremont, California. He asked me to look at the location. I didn't know Fremont as well as I knew Sacramento or San Jose, but I agreed to take a look. When I evaluated the location, I drove around the area ten or fifteen times over a week's period. This allowed me to evaluate traffic flow and discover for myself how it felt driving around there.

In this situation, I told my friend, "Absolutely no, do not build that building. That location does not meet my requirements of a good location for an office building." Meaning, based on what I saw happening in the area, I didn't think my friend would get the type of rent he'd need to cover his costs for developing the project.

He ignored my advice and built anyway. Three years later, the project went bankrupt.

MAKING AN OFFER

Once I had a location determined, I'd make an offer on the land. By this time, I'd made enough profit on my other office buildings in San Jose to be able to pay cash for the Sacramento parcels. If my offer was accepted, and it generally was, I then went to the bank and got a construction loan.

I did everything on my own. I talked to realtors and asked around about potential land for sale. I checked with other businesspeople in the area to see what was happening. I wanted to learn from others, but I didn't want them to know exactly what I was doing.

This isn't to imply that I worked in secret. Word got around about me. I had a reputation as a developer in San Jose, and people in Sacramento soon knew who I was. They knew what I was up to, in general, but I never talked about specific projects until my development was well underway.

This is because other developers were also looking at the same pieces of land. In the case of Point West, there was a complex consisting of three five-story office buildings being developed nearby. The developer of that property was from Los Angeles, and he looked at the same land I was interested in. But he was a large developer, and he had five or six vice presidents and partners with whom he had to consult on what his next step would be. He couldn't make a decision quickly enough. Being a lone operator, I could decide in less than five minutes. One time, the Los Angeles developer called me an investor and a long-term holder. And he said, "Someday, our company would like to be investors like you."

"You can do that," I said. But I was thinking, *who wouldn't want to do that?*

It wasn't so easy for them, though. They had too much overhead. His vice presidents and partners back in Los Angeles all made six figures a year (remember, this is in the late 1970s, when that was quite a sizable salary), and those salaries came out of the company's development budget.

I was generous to the employees who managed my properties; they all made good salaries. But nobody was making six figures working for me in those days, so I didn't have that overhead.

Once I had my process underway, I moved quickly. I didn't want anyone else coming in and buying the land. Again, in the case of Point West, I realized this was prime land. It had freeway access, was close to restaurants, and was even close enough to apartment complexes that people who worked there could walk to and from their jobs.

The way it worked, one day I'd decide what to do, and the next morning I'd be talking to the landowner. I'd have the land in escrow a week later.

KNOW YOUR NUMBERS

I realize that not everyone has this type of vision or work style. I've always been a risk-taker, but my risks are calculated, because I know my costs going in. I always did my own development, so I knew my costs without having to go through a lot of detail with accountants or other consultants.

I knew the tax code well enough to understand what the tax implications would be. I knew my construction costs, within a 5% margin. I knew what the competition was charging for rent in the neighborhood, and I knew that if my property had just the right amount of quality, I could charge more for rent than the competition and still be at capacity, even in a competitive area.

In the evening, I worked out on paper what all my costs would be. In those days, computers were pretty new. You might have a computer at your office, but you certainly weren't carrying around a laptop or a phone. Sometimes I worked on a paper napkin at a restaurant. I was always thinking about business and working out numbers. Because of this, I knew my numbers upfront. All that made it easier for me to make a decision and go forward with a project.

Knowing your numbers is the key to any project's success. You don't want to continually re-estimate the numbers. This is easier now with technology, but I still advise learning math and accounting skills if you plan to run your own business. You can't rely on the computer to think of everything for you. It's a helpful tool, and it makes calculations easier. But you must understand the ins and outs of the numbers, and no computer can do that for you.

ONE AT A TIME

I always developed one project at a time, because as mentioned earlier, I wanted to stay small enough to have control over my projects. If I got too large, I knew I could really fall down. I'd seen it happen to other developers: the overhead gets out of control, and soon you have a bank knocking on your door, wanting money that you haven't yet made on the project.

I also knew that it was much more beneficial and profitable to keep the buildings I developed, rather than selling them. If I kept them, I could avoid paying taxes on capital gains, create income, and take advantage of future appreciation.

I'd learned this lesson early on in my career as a real estate developer. When I first started building in Moline, prior to the development of Townecrest Manor, I built a four-unit apartment building and immediately sold it. After paying all the expenses of the sale and putting aside money for income taxes, I had some money left over. I said to myself, "I need to invest this money. How can I find something to invest in?" Then it dawned on me: I should have simply kept the property I'd sold; I already had an investment in it, and I would have saved the income tax and deferred some expenses. That experience taught me that long-term ownership of real estate is the best way to create wealth.

I always thought long term. When you dream about something you really want to do, you dream about its success. That's just human nature—we all want to see our dreams fulfilled.

Most of us would like to see huge success right from the get-go. But it takes time. Whether it be developing an apartment building, housing development, or whatever you want to get into, make it your point to study your passion inside and out, day and night. Dream about it and sleep on it for a long period of time.

And when the small successes happen, don't take them for granted. Instead, celebrate them, and then move on to the next, bigger thing.

Many people have come to me and said, "I was inspired by you, and I did this and I did that, and my dreams came true." I've known people who built their own buildings like I did, even if they weren't builders, because they wanted a small piece of that industry.

One time, I was having lunch with my attorney. On the side (when he wasn't doing lawyerly things), he was building an apartment building. But there was a lot he didn't know. He asked me about soundproofing and about heating. I told him about those things over lunch. No big deal.

Two weeks later, I got a bill from him for $500 for legal fees, because at that lunch, we were also talking about my business. I sent him a bill back for $550 for helping him soundproof and heat his building.

LOOKING AHEAD: 2083

Point West Commerce Center was completed in 1983. Inside it, we buried a time capsule. The capsule is made of a length of plumbing tube painted gold, and it's buried inside a column in the building. There's a plaque commemorating it. The time capsule is to be opened in the year 2083 or when the building is demolished, whichever comes first.

The time capsule was my idea. These "views into the past" are fairly common in Europe, not as much so in the United States. When I decided to include one in the Point West Commerce Center, I asked local and state politicians to write a letter to put inside it. Four of them did: the Mayor of Sacramento, a City Council member, the County Board of Supervisors Chairman, and the State Senate President Pro Tem.

I love what the 1983 Mayor said, in his letter to the 2083 Mayor: "I almost wrote 'Dear Mr. Mayor,' until I caught myself in the faulty assumption that you will be male. Sacramento has had only one female mayor so far, but I would hope the rate will improve during the next hundred years." Perhaps he was prophetic, because the very next Mayor of Sacramento was a woman, and there has been one more female mayor of that city since then.

As for me, I included pictures of myself, my daughters, and my wife, Angela. I wrote a letter (to whoever wants to read it) explaining my childhood in Germany, how I got my start in the United States, and the successes I'd experienced in Illinois and in California—essentially, much of the same information that's covered in this book, albeit in a much briefer form. I had no idea, when I wrote that letter, that someday I'd write an entire book about my work and my life!

Also in the time capsule are copies of local and national newspapers and magazines, a few coins, and information from the building's subcontractors, detailing their work on the project. There's even a videocassette of a local TV newscast. You have to wonder: in 2083, will they be able to figure out a device that can show it?

Almost forty years have passed since we buried the time capsule. Point West Commerce Center is still thriving, although I don't own it anymore. It will be fascinating, someday, for future generations to open the capsule and pore over the items inside. I hope they enjoy the trip into the past that the time capsule's contents provide.

THE VINEYARDS

While my commercial projects in Sacramento were successful, I didn't limit myself to commercial real estate there. The whole area was booming, and people needed somewhere to live as much as somewhere to work.

I decided that there was a need for homes that were luxurious, but not excessive. I bought a piece of land that had space for fifty homes. Working with a designer who did home floor plans and developments, I came up with a housing concept and a floor plan. Most homes had two bedrooms plus a den, two or three bathrooms, a kitchen, a living room, a dining room, and a two-car garage. They were "garden-style" homes, with spacious, fenced patios and small, landscaped yards with built-in sprinkler systems. The idea was that these would be elegant, private single-family homes, but with a strong sense of community—sort of the feel of a European village. The homes worked for small families, but they also appealed to older couples who wanted the convenience of a condo but the privacy of a single-family home. I decided to call the development The Vineyards.

I built several model homes that people could tour to determine if they were interested in the development. Again, this was done using a construction loan from the bank. I paid cash for the land but borrowed for the construction costs.

This was in the early 1980s, a time of high inflation. When I was well into the project, interest rates soared from 7% to 18% because the Federal Reserve needed to slow down inflation.

With interest rates so high, many people couldn't buy the homes I was building. So, I reached a deal with the bank. I'd buy the interest rate down from 18% to 11% by giving the bank a fee to make up for the shortfall on interest to the bank. That way, the buyer could buy the home at a lower interest rate. Because they could do this, many more people qualified for loans than otherwise would have.

Another development was going up about three miles away from The Vineyards. But that developer had no ability to buy the interest rate down. Instead, he gave the project back to the bank. This is called "in lieu of foreclosure." The bank took the project back and offered an interest rate of 7% to the buyers.

Hearing this, I went to my bank and asked, "Why can't you offer an interest rate at seven, instead of charging eighteen?"

"The other bank took the project back from the developer," they said. "That's why they could do that."

"I'll tell you what," I replied. "Why don't you take my project back, too? Then you can offer a lower interest rate to the buyers. I can't subsidize these interest rates forever. I'm just a small operator." My bank agreed and took the project back in lieu of foreclosure.

They did that because that was preferable to having the project go bankrupt.

That wasn't an ideal outcome, but it's an example of how sometimes things happen that are outside our control. The dramatic rise in interest rates was unexpected, and a lot of businesses took a hit because of it. There wasn't anything I could do about it, other than put it behind me and move on to the next thing.

KNOW YOUR BUSINESS

A bit more on the situation above. If there had been a foreclosure, it would have been for only that project, not for my entire corporation. That's because I did each project under a different LLC (limited liability company). This way, if things don't work out as planned, as happened with The Vineyards, it didn't affect my personal finances or my other properties. Each project stood on its own financially.

I always set up LLCs, because they're ongoing. An LLC allows you to add several extra investors, down the line. With a corporation, that's a bit more difficult. Also, if you want to give some of your projects to your children or to other people, with an LLC, it's just a matter of legal documentation, and you give them whatever percentage of the project you choose.

This may be surprising, but I like to set up my LLCs in Delaware. Why? Because Delaware has the most stringent laws of protection on the owner of a corporation or LLC.

California has a very high state income tax. By contrast, Washington State has no state income tax. (More about Washington later.) These days, I live in Arizona, which has a very low state income tax. This is something I've taken into consideration in deciding where to live, over the years. Knowing how a state's income tax compares to other states' taxes can help with your financial planning.

How do I know all this? I made it my point to learn. I found out everything I could about accounting. If you don't know what's going on in the accounting world, then you're at the will of somebody else's plans.

Accountants are good at what they do (some of them, anyway), but they aren't entrepreneurs. They're tax people; they're businesspeople. Their job is to keep the books.

My job, always, was to know my business inside out, to know my numbers, and to understand what could and what might happen. That way, even when things took a negative turn, as they did for me with The Vineyards, I was able to come back from that with relative ease.

A PRODUCTIVE ERA

Those years developing properties in Sacramento were fruitful, satisfying ones. I enjoyed every moment of my time in that business, from scouting locations to working out the financing, developing the project, and seeing tenants and homeowners enjoying and appreciating the properties I'd built.

So did I keep going? You might, logically, think I did. If so, you'd be surprised. I was far from retirement, but I *was* ready to try something completely different.

I decided it was time for my professional life to take a drastic turn. I thought, *I should start my own bank.*

CHALLENGE YOURSELF

•   How has your personal life affected your business life, and vice versa? In what ways can you balance your personal and professional lives?

•   Have you ever scouted a location for a prospective business or other venture? What was the experience like? Would you do it again?

•   If you're thinking of starting your own business, do you want a partner? Why or why not?

•   Do you tend to act quickly, or do you take your time before making a decision and acting on it? In what ways has your approach benefited or hindered you in the past?

•   Have you ever been part of a time capsule project? If you were asked to contribute something for a time capsule, what would that item be?

•   If you've ever had a project take an unexpectedly adverse turn, what did you do to curtail your loss?

•   What steps have you taken (or do you plan to take) to mini mize potential future setbacks in your business?

My childhood home in Shaudbill, Germany, built in 1901. I took this photo in around 2011.

3511 15th Street, Moline, IL. I built this home myself, working in the evenings and on the weekends, for myself and my bride, Elke.

Elke and me, featured in the Moline Dispatch, December 1955, in the kitchen of our home that I built. The caption called the home, "YOUNG PEOPLE'S DREAM!"

Glistening Array of New Homes Will Be on Parade

By PETER H. PAULSEN
General Chairman Parade of Homes

The Quad-City Parade of Homes, Sept. 30 through Oct. 7, rings up the curtain on a drama close to the hearts of American families — the drama of new homes.

PETER H. PAULSEN

Moline Dispatch, September 1962. As chairman of the Parade of Homes committee, I was asked to be a guest editor, writing a piece about the Parade for the newspaper.

AIR CONDITIONING

How To Hide An Air Conditioner

There are all sorts of tricks and manners and ways to hide your air conditioner. At left is one of the more clever innovations. Mrs. Peter Paulsen of 3730 19th Ave, Moline, is shown by a slightly protruding area in her paneled family room which conceals the room's air conditioner. A large clock aids the camouflage.

Many Quad-Citians have found it practical to use louvered shutters to hide their air conditioners, while others have used cloth draperies, match stick curtains, etc.

Quad-City Times, September 1962. The home I built for the Parade of Homes, at 3730 19th Avenue, Moline, was a showstopper. Here, Elke demonstrates how their air conditioner was disguised behind a wall panel. We liked that house so much, after the Parade, we decided to move our family in to it.

Towncrest Manor, the first apartment complex I ever built. I completed the complex in 1962. This present-day photo is evidence of how well-built the complex is. Towncrest Manor is now condominiums.

Paulsen Manor, my second Moline apartment complex. I sold this complex decades ago, but it's still called Paulsen Manor and there is still a waiting list to rent there.

Golds, oranges, and greens provide warmth to the Paulsens' spacious living room.

designed for comfort and convenience . . . styled in a choice of color combinations, equipped with the latest GE Mark 27 ranges with 21" ovens . . . birch cabinets . . . formica countertops . . . deluxe vinyl floor coverings requiring a minimum of maintenance. Large sinks with disposal units.

For your further comfort, the construction is planned to offer complete sound-proofing with heavy wall insulation coupled with apartment layout techniques developed to isolate sounds of operating equipment or noise. Central air conditioning

provided in the front of each apartment for your own Christmas decorations.

Paulsen Manor has provided a private swimming and recreation area perfectly planned and located away from the living area. Recreation building complete with kitchen facilities may be used by the tenants for a nominal fee. Ideal for wedding receptions, card parties, etc.

NOTICE: All plans and contents of brochure are property of PETER PAULSEN CONSTRUCTION CO. and will be unlawful to copy or reproduce without authorized consent of owner.

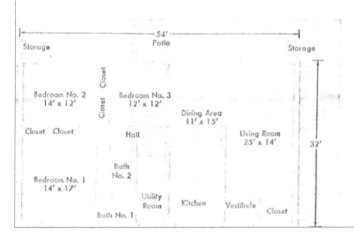

3 Bedroom Deluxe

A paragon of luxurious living . . . this deluxe apartment sparkles with new ideas . . . ingeniously designed to stimulate creative arrangements for entertaining, privacy, or both simultaneously. A spacious 17' x 14-1/2' master bedroom with full bathroom adjoining, plus full bath accessible for other rooms . . . wall-to-wall closets . . . "L" shaped living room and dining area creates spacious feeling, yet can be divided to suit any occasion. See it soon and delight in its atmosphere of sophisticated, easy living.

Page 1 of the original sales brochure for Paulsen Manor, showing the floor plan for a 3 bedroom deluxe apartment.

Villa Del Prado

Quad City Times, January 1966 For a while, my family and I lived in a 3 bedroom deluxe unit at Paulsen Manor. The local paper did a 4 page spread about our spacious apartment, which felt more like a house than some houses do. One of the captions said "You hardly believe it's an apartment."

A rendering of the Villa del Prado apartment complex, which I built in San Jose, CA in 1970

The front cover of the Homebuilding's Apartment Report, June 1970 which included a 5 page feature (and front cover photo) about Villa del Prado

Four Villa Del Prado floor plans offer 6 by 12-ft. balconies. Some two-bedroom, two-bath models have central living rooms with bedrooms on either side to appeal to bachelor residents who are "doubling up."

Villa del Prado layouts. Many of the 2-bedroom, 2-bath units feature a central living room and kitchen with the bedrooms to the sides, providing privacy for roommates sharing the unit. The complex, now called The Monterey, still stands and is still apartments.

PROFILE

Of A Successful Business Park

Peter Paulsen

Several years ago, in 1972 our company had just completed and sold the Villa del Prado apartment complex, and was looking for a new market in the form of real estate investments. A quick survey made by our company revealed that there was going to be an ever increasing demand for office space.

We started one building, 4100 Moorpark Avenue, on a trial basis. This building reached 100% occupancy within a very short period of time. At that time we purchased the adjoining property and built a slightly larger building. Again, it reached full occupancy in a very short time period.

I then decided to go ahead and purchase and option the adjoining land for additional office space. Since that time we have completed one new building every year. At this time, Paulsen Office Park, on Moorpark Avenue, just east of Saratoga Avenue, consists of 130,000 square feet, with an additional 46,000 square feet scheduled for completion by the end of 1979, making a total of 170,000 square feet located on 9 acres.

We handle all our own design work, as well as construction. At the beginning of the complex we tried to get away from the sterile

A feature piece about my office park on Moorpark Avenue in San Jose, in Today's Real Estate, April 1979

Point West Commerce Center. Notice the sign for Commerce Security Bank on the side of the building.

Rendering of the 21,000 square foot (including basement) home that I built in Hillsboro, CA. I had planned to live in this house but never did; instead deciding to move to Montecito, CA. Joe

Montana, the San Francisco 49ers quarterback, wanted to buy the house; but unfortunately, another buyer already had it under contract. The house is now worth about $30 million.

A flyer for The Vineyards, the "garden-style homes" I developed in Sacramento

The back of the Hillsboro, CA home

A vacation home I built for myself in Newport Beach, CA

The Freya, choked in Vancouver, BC

Aerial view of the Hotel Bellwether.

The lighthouse at the Hotel Bellwether.

A view of Squalicum Harbor, showing the Hotel Bellwether.

The Freya docked at the Hotel Bellwether.

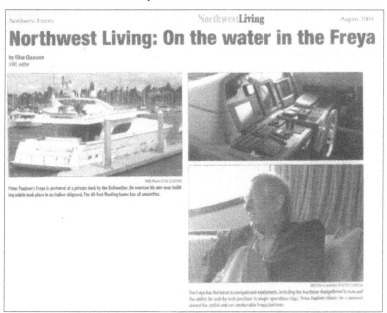

An August 2004 article about the last boat I owned, an 80-foot Ferretti.

Peter Paulsen Stage

My previous home in Phoenix, which I built in 1998

Denis and my current Phoenix home. When we bought this house, we downsized going from

Paulsen's fondness for Bellingham led to a $50 million gift

BY DAVE GALLAGHER
dgallagher@bhamherald.com

Bellingham is fortunate that Peter Paulsen saw its potential nearly 25 years ago.

Paulsen, who recently donated $50 million to expand Bellingham's PeaceHealth St. Joseph Medical Center, was pondering retirement in the late 1990s after a successful career in construction and real estate.

Peter Paulsen

He was living in the San Francisco Bay Area and had just sold a bank.

"I was looking for a smaller town and found Bellingham," said Paulsen, 87, in a telephone interview with The Bellingham Herald. Now living in Phoenix, he noted that the size of Bellingham reminded him of some

Design concept for a future proposed Peter Paulsen Pavilion at PeaceHealth St. Joseph Medical Center in Bellingham.

of the towns in Germany, his childhood home, with the added bonus of being on the water.
After moving to Bellingham,

Paulsen, who had tried retirement before but it never

SEE PAULSEN, 4A

Dear Mr. & Mrs. Paulson,

Thank you for your extraordinary gesture of support & trust in our local community hospital. Your extraordinary gift will positively impact the health and wellness of innumerable Whatcom county residents and Washingtonians. I serve as the Chief Medical Officer, and I have spoken with many community physicians and we all are humbled and grateful for your support.

Thank you,
Sudhakar Karlapudi

Dear Mr. Paulsen   02/15/2022

I write to thank you for your recent
unbelieveable gift to PeaceHealth St. Joseph
Medical Center and our expansion plan! In
all my years in healthcare across our great
country, I have never seen an individual
donation such as yours. Thank you, while
powerful words, seem inadequate. For me, your
gift will enable us to plan for those design and/
or equipment elements that will transform the
Paulsen Pavilion to a world-class tower of care
and service. Thank you for your world-class
    generosity!
                              Elliot Knide
                              NWN COO

A recent photo of Diana and me.

Dana and the beside a NetJets plane. We love the convenience of the NetJets service

Happy together: Dana and her

CHAPTER 10

PETER PAULSEN, BANKER
(1984 – 1994)

MY NEXT VENTURE

My idea to get involved in the banking industry actually dates back before I even developed the Point West office complex in Sacramento. In the early 1980s, I was asked to be on the board of directors for a small business bank in San Jose, California. This deal required me to buy $300,000 worth of stock in that bank. When I did so, I joined the board and also became chairman of the loan committee at that bank, since I had a thorough understanding of how business financing worked. But I didn't like the way that bank was being run. Eventually I got out of the deal. I determined that instead, I'd start my own bank.

Since I was still working primarily in Sacramento, I decided toestablish a bank in that city. This was around the time of the savings and loan (S&L) collapse. Due to substantial inflation in the late 1970s, hundreds of S&L institutions, many of them small, local businesses, had been making bad loans. They were in trouble financially, and the Federal Deposit Insurance Corporation (FDIC) prohibited them from making new loans. Most of these institutions permanently shut their doors.

That's when I started my bank. We started the bank as an S&L, but because our bank was new and had no history, it held no bad loans. Therefore, regulators permitted our bank to make new loans. We also started with the idea that not all of our loans would be for residential properties. We would also do commercial loans. Because of the S&L crisis, the federal government had passed laws that allowed S&Ls to offer more commercial lending. My thought was that doing both commercial and residential lending would help insulate the bank from the ups and downs of the residential lending market.

AGAIN, RESEARCH IS VITAL

How did I know what to do before I opened the bank? I knew because I studied it. Just as I'd done when I wanted to get into real estate development, I read every book and article about banking that I could get my hands on. I also met with a banking regulator in San Francisco to make sure I understood what was required. I attended banking education seminars geared toward managers of banks. I learned everything they could teach me at those seminars. I went to banking seminars in New York, Chicago, and elsewhere in the country. I flew all over to attend banking seminars hosted by the American Bankers Association, of which I was a member long before I started a bank. At the seminars, I learned about certain bankers' successes, so I could emulate them—as well as about other bankers' mistakes, so I wouldn't make those mistakes myself. Using all this research, I put together a thorough, solid business plan for starting my bank.

You can learn about any industry, but you have to put in the time doing your research. You must study it and read about it, and you must continue to do so, because things change. I've always been interested in the financial news, but when I began to consider going into banking, I started reading the financial news voraciously. I subscribed to banking newspapers and magazines, and I read them cover to cover, so I'd know what was happening in the industry.

I kept those subscriptions and maintained those reading habits the entire time I owned my bank, and beyond. Whatever your industry is, if you want to be an entrepreneur, you have to study it constantly. You can't simply ignore your industry's news and trends. If you do, you'll be left behind. Or worse, you'll make irreparable mistakes.

While I was doing all that studying and learning, I also thought about the best location for my bank. It turned out that the perfect spot was within the project I was already constructing: the Point West office complex.

My daughter, Susan, says, "My dad was a master extrapolating in his mind the future potential of land or property, assuming the risk of the cost and the lag in time for that area to develop. In Sacramento, he built Point West and decided to put his bank there. That area was at a freeway off-ramp. When he first built there, not much nearby was developed. But within very little time, the commercial development of that area erupted, and he was already established there, like a cornerstone. He excelled at being in the right place at the right time." We decided to open the bank on the first floor of the Point West Commerce Center, with administrative offices on the second floor.

We named our new bank Commerce Security Bank.

WHO IS THIS "WE?"

You may have noticed that I've been mentioning "we" in regard to the bank and, as I've already established in this book, I prefer to be a lone operator. So perhaps you're wondering: who is this "we" that was involved in opening Commerce Security Bank?

The answer is simple: they were my board of directors. Every bank needs a board of directors because people who put their money into a banking institution want assurance that no single person has complete control over their finances.

When considering who should be on my board of directors, I came up with several criteria:

• **Stock ownership**. There was no requirement (neither federal nor state) that my directors *had* to own stock in the bank. But I wanted them to own stock. I knew that if my board of directors owned shares in Commerce Security Bank, they'd be more invested in its success. That said, I wanted to own the majority of shares. At the bank in San Jose where I'd been a director, the principle who started it only owned 10% of shares. I knew I wanted a much larger share than that. My six directors would each own 1%, while I retained 94% ownership.

• **Business-oriented**. I wanted my directors to be businesspeople. I knew that people with business-oriented minds and backgrounds would be more likely to comprehend the ins and outs of the banking business.

• **Business relationships only**. While I've always had many friends in the business world, I didn't want the stockholders of my bank to be friends of mine. Mixing business and friendship can cloud relationships, and I wasn't willing to risk having that happen.

• **No "yes-people."** I didn't want people on the board who had no opinions of their own, people who just agreed with everything that everyone else said. I wanted bright, hardworking businesspeople who would be invested in the bank's success.

I selected a group of six and asked them to join me as directors. To each of them, I said, "You've got to own 1% of the stock."

They all reviewed my business plan. They all felt it was a strong plan, and the bank was likely to be a success. As a result, all six accepted my offer to join the board.

The amount needed to establish the bank was $4.2 million. I put $3,600,000 into the kitty, which represented 96% ownership. With a $100,000 investment, each of the other six directors had 1% ownership.

Starting a bank is like any other business deal. You develop the business to make a profit. Our intention was to make money, and then somewhere down the line, sell the bank for a large profit.

UP AND RUNNING

Once I had the location established and the directors on board, we began the regulatory process needed to open the bank. This involved the California Department of Savings and Loan: to do background checks on all the board members and me, review the financial status of the project, and thoroughly examine my two-year business plan. In addition to comprehensively describing the bank project, the business plan was required to demonstrate a need in the community for our bank. Because I'd done so much research and put so much time into developing a solid business plan, and because I'd so carefully selected the people who were on the board of directors, we had no trouble getting through the 90-day regulatory process.

I made myself chairman of the board, chairman of the loan committee, and an ex-officio member of all the committees, so I was very much involved. For my president, I hired a banking consultant from San Francisco who'd worked for the huge accounting firm Peat, Marwick, & Mitchell. He was a bright young man with lots of banking background. He was a brilliant bank president, and he implemented many excellent programs for Commerce Security Bank.

Together, my new president and I hired the rest of the staff, including excellent people to work on the mortgage side. Because so many other banks were in trouble, a lot of talented people in the industry were being laid off. Numerous well-qualified savings and loan people were looking for a job and for a change.

As mentioned, Commerce Security Bank started as a savings and loan that handled both residential and commercial loans. After a year, we converted it to a business bank.

From the start, we did a lot of commercial loans. Even though S&Ls could now do commercial loans, many of them were, as I noted earlier, prohibited by the regulators from making new loans because they had bad loans on the books. All the businesspeople who couldn't get a loan from another bank came to us, and we got all that business.

We also did plenty of residential loans. In 1985, at the height of the market, we did $90 million a month of refinances on residential properties. After interest rates came down substantially, people were eager to refinance.

We made no loans to the directors and no loans to me. Because banks are regulated by the FDIC, you don't want to play favoritism to yourself with money from your own bank.

What we *did* do was finance a lot of homes and businesses that other banks were not able to, because the FDIC prohibited them from making new loans until they got their balance sheets back in order.

I was chairman of the loan committee. That worked in the bank's favor because I have a nose for a bad deal. When people wanted to rip me off, I could always tell.

By this point in my life and my career, I knew my own strengths very well. If I wasn't the right person to chair the loan committee, I wouldn't have done it. In that case, I would have put someone else in that position instead.

If you're going to be an entrepreneur, it's important that you don't let ego get in the way of doing what's right for your business. I knew there were some aspects of running the bank that were better suited to other people's skill sets than mine. I let them handle those tasks, and I concentrated on the aspects at which I excelled.

SELLING THE BANK

In 1996, I sold Commerce Security Bank in a merger deal with another bank in Southern California. Both banks would be owned under a parent company and would continue to operate independently. With the merger, I cashed out most of my shares. We'd started with $4 million in assets, and when Commerce Security Bank was sold, it had $250 million in assets. It was, at the time, the fourth largest locally based bank in Sacramento. The sale generated a profit of about $10 million

You might wonder why I sold such a profitable business. I'd enjoyed owning it, but it took a lot of time, and my heart wasn't in it for the long term. The only way to grow it would have been to start a banking chain, and I wasn't interested in doing that.

Besides, for me, starting a new project is much more fun than owning it. This is why I often sold a building in order to develop a new one, or to do something else.

Same thing with the bank. By the time I'd owned it for over a decade, I was ready to move on.

Of course, that's just me. Everyone is different, and some people like to start a new project or a business and stick with it for decades, perhaps for the rest of their lives. The important thing is to know *yourself* well enough to know how you, personally, operate. When you understand yourself, you can better plan for the future—both your business's and your own.

CHALLENGE YOURSELF

•   Have you ever completely shifted gears, going into an entirely different line of work? If so, what research did you conduct before making the shift? How did it work out?

•   If you're considering starting a business, have you written a business plan? This is a vital step in any entrepreneurial effort.

•   If you had to work with a group (such as a board of directors), what criteria would you have for group membership?

•   Do you have dreams that you're hesitant to work toward? If so, consider what's holding you back.

•   If you have started a business or are considering doing so, what is your end game? How long do you expect to own the business? If you plan to someday sell your business, what plans have you made for the eventual sale?

CHAPTER 11

A NEW PHASE IN MY LIFE
(1996 – 20 08)

JUGGLING BUSINESS AND PERSONAL LIFE

During the years I was running the bank, I still lived in Montecito and commuted every week or two to Sacramento. I had to be there for board meetings, which happened once a month. But I preferred to be at the bank more often. Generally, I stayed in Sacramento for three or four days at a time.

The bank president I'd hired did an excellent job running Commerce Security Bank on a day-to-day basis. And I did a lot of work on the telephone. Computers were becoming more commonplace, but email was not yet a common method of communication. We did everything via telephone, fax, and being in person.

I didn't mind that. In fact, I enjoyed being at the bank. I liked to see my bank operation firsthand, so I spent a lot of time going back and forth from Montecito to Sacramento.

In the late 1980s, when Angela and I had been married for about a decade, we decided to adopt. We put our names in at an adoption agency, and finally we reached the top of the list. The biological mother of our child was 17 years old and enrolled in a church program. She lived in a dormitory with other women in the same situation. We met her and talked, and we said that if she'd accept us, we'd like to adopt her child. After she agreed, her attorney interviewed us. Then we were approved to become the parents of her baby when it was born. She had a boy, and we were there for his birth. We named him Peter Andreas Paulsen.

Two years later, the same young woman was pregnant again and wanted to put the child up for adoption. Angela and I said, "We must keep these siblings together. Let's adopt this one, too." The biological mother was pleased with this plan, knowing her kids would be raised together. She had a girl, whom we adopted and named Lauren Paulsen.

By this point, I was in my late fifties, and my older three daughters were all living their adult lives. I even had grandchildren. You might think that would make me dismiss the idea of raising more kids. But I was still healthy, fit, and energetic. And I believe kids keep you young. I saw no reason not to become a parent again at this point in my life.

This is a lesson about the adage, "It's never too late," which I believe wholeheartedly. If there's something you want—whether it's a new business venture, relocation, a new partner, or a family—then age should not hold you back from pursuing your dreams.

SOME THINGS ENDURE, WHILE OTHERS CHANGE

It's important to note that all the years I was in the banking business, it wasn't my total business. I still had my office developments and other properties. I had the commercial developments in Sacramento and San Jose. Altogether, it was probably a little over 200,000 square feet of office space. That's a small number as far as developers go, but it was a big number for me.

All of that was managed through my business, the Peter Paulsen Company. I had employees, of course, who managed leasing, advertising and sales, and maintenance of my properties. But I built all my office buildings for long-term holding, and I was still invested in the day-to-day operations of them. I wanted to know what was going on, and I made it my business to do so.

All that time, my personal residence was in Montecito. Angela and I loved the town, and I didn't mind the commute. We were in Montecito when we adopted Peter and Lauren. I also kept a place in San Mateo, not far from San Jose. I stayed there when I was working in Northern California.

In 1995, Angela and I got divorced. It was the same thing that had happened with Elke; I was simply working much more than my wife wanted me to. Especially when I owned the bank, the banking regulators required me to be in Sacramento at specific, frequent times. You can't run a bank remotely.

Initially, it wasn't a problem, but over time, it really raised hell with my marriage.

But working like that is simply what I'm wired to do. By this time, I knew myself well enough to understand this truth. I was driven to work that way, and I did enjoy my work and found it rewarding. But working that much definitely took a toll on my personal relationships.

The brutal truth is, no individual is capable of doing everything. Each of us is only granted twenty-four hours per day, and we all have to make choices about how to use our twenty-four hours. I realize now that in my first two marriages, I chose business over the relationship—and while sometimes I have regrets about that, I can't go back and change it.

But I can learn from it. I'm now retired from real estate investing and banking. I live in Phoenix with my wife, Diana, and work on my stock portfolio full time, from my laptop in my home office. It's a very different lifestyle than I had back then, but I enjoy every minute of it. My current lifestyle is extremely rewarding for me.

It's a lesson in understanding what's important to you and recognizing that you're only human. If you want to be an entrepreneur, you will have to devote incredible amounts of time to work. Every successful entrepreneur I've ever known has had to face this truth, and so have those entrepreneurs' spouses and families.

It's something to consider as you think about starting a business: do you have the time to devote to making it a success? I can't answer that for you, of course, but I do urge you to think carefully about it. When we divorced, Angela and I agreed to a joint custody arrangement. That meant I had Peter and Lauren with me a lot of the time. Sometimes, I had them all summer.

By this time, I'd sold the bank, which, ironically, gave me more time to devote to my personal life, at exactly the moment when I was no longer married. The silver lining is that it also gave me a lot of time to devote to my kids. I was very actively involved when Peter and Lauren were young. Kids *should* take priority; this is another universal truth. If you're a parent, you never get that time back with your kids. You need to treasure it and make the most of it.

In the ensuing years, while Peter and Lauren were growing up, I spent a lot of time with them. I took them out on my boat, which I kept in Washington State. We would fly up there and go boating. I taught them how to ride bicycles. I taught them how to swim and dive. I truly was busy raising those kids.

Because of this, I didn't have much time for romance. It's hard to date when you have young kids, so I essentially put that part of my life on hold for a while.

It might not have been the family life that, when I was a young man, I'd have envisioned for myself when I was in my sixties. But it had many positive moments. I enjoyed the time I was able to spend with all five of my kids, as well as with my grandkids. When it comes to family, I've always considered myself extremely lucky.

WHAT'S NEXT?

After the bank sale and my second divorce, I had to do some soulsearching to figure out what I wanted next. At 61 years old, I was the owner of a successful commercial real estate company and the previous owner of a bank (one who had walked away from the deal with a considerable profit). I was also a single dad of two young kids. Where did I want to go, and what would I do there?

I decided to give Phoenix, Arizona a try. Phoenix is a city I'd always loved, on my many visits there. I enjoyed the warm, dry climate and the people I met. It seemed like a place with a lot going on, so I knew there would be plenty of opportunity. I bought a lot in Phoenix and built a house on it. I moved both my personal and business lives to Phoenix, near Paradise Valley. By this time, I also had a house in Bellingham, Washington, which I kept until I had completed all my business endeavors on the West Coast.

After I'd spent a lot of time in Phoenix, I started looking around to see what I might be able to develop. I could have done more commercial development, but I wanted to try something new. A lot of shopping centers were being built, and I determined that my next business venture would be shopping centers. In a city like that, with lots of retirees and very warm weather (especially in the summer months), people spent significant time—

and money—escaping the heat by going shopping. I could see that retail was thriving in Phoenix, and I wanted to be a part of it.

This is another lesson in paying attention to what a community desires and where they want it. Just as I had in Sacramento and other areas when I scoped out a location for a new commercial development, in Phoenix I scoped out the city and found that what was most desired were opportunities for shopping. I'm not much of a shopper myself, but that doesn't matter; what matters is what works for the community.

If you want to be in business, it's important not only to do something that interests you—that's a given—but also something that addresses a want or a need in your community. Identifying the want or need first is key to entrepreneurial success.

SHOPPING CENTERS

To get into the shopping center business, I sold some of my office buildings in San Jose and Sacramento, and I did a 1031 exchange. A 1031 exchange means you sell your property and put the capital into another property. When you do that, if what you buy is worth more than what you sold, you don't have to pay taxes on the capital gains. Instead, you defer the gains into the future. When you do this, it's important to understand the tax code and pay attention to what's available to do as an investor, such as building depreciation and equipment depreciation for items like elevators, HVAC, and carpeting.

I used 1031 exchanges to buy two shopping centers in the Phoenix suburb of Scottsdale. Both were existing projects, about a year old, in an up-and-coming area. Again: location, location, location.

Each of my two shopping centers was 100,000 square feet, meaning I owned 200,000 square feet of retail space in Scottsdale. One of them was at Pinnacle Peak Road and Pima Road, and it was anchored by an AJ's Fine Foods and a CVS drugstore. The balance of the project consisted of a lot of small "mom-and-pop" shops. The second one was similar, a couple of good anchor stores and a lot of smaller shops.

When I bought those properties, the structures were built, but neither project was completely rented yet. I did what's called the "rental phase for the developer." What this did was guarantee the rent as if each unit was rented, until it actually was rented. The developer paid the rent on the vacant spaces until they were rented. As each unit was rented, the developer phased out of the project.

I ran those shopping centers myself. As with all my previous ventures, I always ran my own business. I interviewed and hired my own property managers, so I knew who was working for me and how they were managing my holdings.

As far as leasing went, 90% of the leases for those shopping centers were done in-house. Quite often, people simply walked into the office wanting to rent space. We had an office on-site at each shopping center. We also offered to pay a real estate commission to any broker who brought us a qualified tenant.

You might wonder, since I had so much experience building new projects, why I didn't build new shopping centers. The answer goes back to the above: location. I looked around at undeveloped land, but I didn't see any sites that had as much potential as the two shopping centers that were already under development and were for sale.

This was simply a common-sense way to approach the business.

Yes, I could have developed my own shopping centers, but there was no reason to. It's another lesson in being flexible in order to achieve success.

RECESSION

For over a decade, things went well. I built my house and divided my time between Phoenix and Washington State, where I kept my boat. I traveled to California for business, as required, as well as to see my older daughters and their families.

I enjoyed spending time in Phoenix, and my shopping centers continued to thrive. In addition to the shopping centers, I bought a couple of small office buildings in Phoenix. Over time, I shifted my operations from Sacramento and San Jose investments to Phoenix investments.

Then, in 2008-2009, the recession hit. Everything went down. Interest rates went so low, it was almost like free money—taken from my stock portfolio, which I used as collateral to buy more stocks, selling at a 50% discount.

(Much more about that later in this book.) I didn't like the way things were going, so I sold my Phoenix office buildings. At the same time, I was operating my shopping centers with property managers in-house, and we noticed that the "mom-and-pop" operators who rented space from us were beginning to have difficulty making their rent. The internet was exploding, and suddenly you could buy anything and everything online. The recession also meant that many people were struggling to make ends meet, and as a result, they were looking for the best bargain they could find, which often meant buying the item from an online retailer. All of that took sales away from the small brick-and-mortar operators, like those in my shopping centers.

The writing was on the wall. I decided it was time to get out of the shopping center business. This is what happens sometimes. When I went into that business in the late 1990s, it was a great time to own shopping centers. But things change, and you have to pay attention, and you have to keep up. Everything changed on the business approach to shopping centers because the buying public changed its way of purchasing goods. That change put a lot of small operators out of business. I felt bad for them, but I hope that they, too, were keeping up with what was going on in their own respective industries. The ones who were forward-thinking likely learned how to move their business either partially or fully online.

When I sold the shopping centers in Scottsdale, the stock market had gone down substantially as a result of the recession. Most large companies were selling shares at fifty cents on the dollar. I invested the proceeds from the sale of the shopping centers into stocks with an A+ rating and a high dividend payout.

I could talk about stocks all day long. They became my passion, and they remain my passion to this day. But I'll leave that topic for later in this book.

Instead, in the following few chapters, I'll shift gears a bit and talk about what I loved to do (and still love to do) when I'm *not* working.

CHALLENGE YOURSELF

• Think about times you've had to start over, either personally, professionally, or both. What did you decide to do? What drove your decision-making?

• How do you balance your personal and professional lives? If you want to start a business, what steps will you take to ensure your personal relationships don't suffer?

- If you're thinking about starting a business, have you considered what need or desire it meets in your community? (Keep in mind that if your business will be run primarily online, your "community" could be internet users.)

- If your business begins to wane, what steps will you take to either adapt the business or sell it and move on?

CHAPTER 12

ALL WORK AND NO PLAY? HARDLY!

MY "LEISURE" TIME

The previous chapters in this book might make it sound as if I've always worked 24/7. But that's simply not true. As I mentioned at the end of the last chapter, I'd like to shift the discussion a bit and talk about what I do when I'm not working. I'll devote the next several chapters to some of my nonwork passions.

READ ANY GOOD BOOKS LATELY?

This question comes up quite a bit, doesn't it? As I'm working on *this* book, it's summertime. For many people, that means vacation. People spend long days on the beach, camped out on towels under sun umbrellas, sipping something cold and watching the waves. Many enjoy light reading during such vacation times, novels that aren't too hefty, for instance, the type of book that's often called (by advertisers, anyway) the "perfect beach read."

I guess it depends on who you are. When I go to the beach, my perfect beach reads are:

- *U.S. News & World Report*
- *Forbes*
- *Fortune*
- *The Wall Street Journal*
- *Newsweek*

- *Financial Times*

- *USA Today* (for general news and the financial section)

I don't read the Sports section. I never was involved in sports. I didn't have time for sports, nor interest in following them.

I've never read a lot of fiction. I know there are good novels out there, but that type of reading has never captured my interest the way nonfiction does. But I find it relaxing and enjoyable (as well as intellectually stimulating) to read articles in the above-mentioned periodicals, all of which I subscribe to and read regularly. I like to know what's happening in the business and financial worlds. I've been reading this type of material for decades.

As an example, in the late 1980s, when I owned Commerce Security Bank, there was a Swiss company interested in buying the bank. My bank president and I flew to Switzerland to meet with representatives from that company. It was a twelve-hour trip on the way back. I spent the entire flight reading business journals, business magazines, and business books. My bank manager read novels. He said he liked "escapist" reading when he traveled.

Don't misunderstand me: there's nothing wrong with that type of reading if it's what you love. The important thing is to find what *your* passion is. For me, I don't get much out of reading novels. I've read several with decent business theory in them, but those are few and far between.

I like reading nonfiction books because the lessons are usually concrete and discernable. I get a lot out of the nonfiction I read. Some of my favorite books are:

- *The Millionaire Next Door* by Thomas J. Stanley (1996). This book profiles a number of American millionaires.

- *Rich Dad Poor Dad* by Robert Kiyosaki and Sharon Lechter (1997). I love this one because it explains the importance of financial literacy and how you can build wealth through investments and business ownership.

- *Why We Want You to Be Rich: Two Men, One Message* (2006). Again by Robert Kiyosaki, this time co-authored with Donald Trump, this book explains building wealth through real estate investment.

- (As an aside, Robert Kiyosaki is now my next-door neighbor in

Phoenix. It was wonderful to be able to tell him in person how inspirational I find his books to be!)

• *Think Like a Billionaire* by Donald Trump (2005). In this book, Trump discusses his "billionaire mindset."

• *Real Estate 101: Building Wealth with Real Estate Investment* by Gary W. Eldred, Forward by Donald Trump (2006). This is part of the Trump University series, and it explains Trump's methodology for real estate investing.

• *Megatrends 2010* by Patricia Aburdene (2010). Aburdene also co-authored the bestselling *Megatrends 2000*. In this 2010 volume, she investigates corporate social responsibility, identifying megatrends that she envisioned would redefine business in the coming years. It's interesting to read this book now, over a decade later, to see what held true and what didn't. I think it's important to be future focused in your reading. I call this "reading the future," and it's something I love to do.

• *Protect and Enhance Your Estate: Definitive Strategies for Estate and Wealth Planning,* by Robert A. Esperti, Renno L. Peterson, and David K. Cahoone (2012). Over the years, as my estate grew, I've always known it was important to understand how to protect it. This book provides practical steps for protecting your estate, no matter its size. As with many subjects, when it comes to estate planning and management, you need to know enough to ask the right questions, to put it in the proper perspective for your own planning. Otherwise, you (or your heirs) will end up handing over too much to the government. I'd rather give my money to charity (and some of it to my kids).

Finally, I sure would love to tell you the title of the book I read in the 1950s about apartment-building development and management. I'd certainly like to thank the authors of that book if I could. Their slim but information-packed volume was life changing for me. But as I mentioned earlier, I can't remember the title of that book—and long ago, my copy was lost in the shuffle of moving.

If you want to be an entrepreneur, it's important to read business books and periodicals that will help you get started. It's also vital to read material related to your specific industry. This is one way to stay on top of trends.

Whatever your reading passion is, I hope you're a reader. Books and magazines provide windows into other worlds. We're fortunate to have them available to us, which is another benefit of living in a free country like the United States. When I was growing up in Germany, most of our reading material was what the government put in front of us. In the U.S., we're all free to read whatever we want. It's a freedom that shouldn't be taken for granted.

CARE TO DANCE?

As I mentioned in Chapter 3, I learned how to dance as a youth in Germany. That required curriculum is something that has truly stayed with me and benefited me for my entire life. Elke and I hit it off in that German club in Moline because we both loved dancing. If you think about it, I wouldn't have the family I have now, my kids and grandkids, if dancing hadn't started it all. My current wife, Diana, is an amazing dancer as well.

My passion for dancing continued well past the years when Elke and I were together, and it continues to this day. As mentioned, Diana also loves to dance. Like me, Diana was raised in Europe—she grew up in Bulgaria—and like me, she learned to dance as part of her schooling. She knows how to waltz, and that's one of our favorite dances to do. Often, Diana and I get applause when we're dancing. Even if we're in a restaurant that only has room for about five or six couples to dance by the piano, we're out there on the floor.

If you've never considered yourself much of a dancer, I encourage you to at least give it a try. If you're self-conscious, you might consider taking lessons. Dancing is fun, social, and good exercise. I think everyone should learn to dance.

EUROPEAN TRAVEL

Diana and I also like to travel. We've been all over the United States together. We haven't been to Europe together because of the pandemic, but soon, we're planning to do that. We'd especially like to go to Bulgaria and Italy together. Whenever I've traveled to Europe, I've flown first class on British Airways to London, and then on to wherever I wanted to go on the continent.

I've made many trips to Italy. Partly, those trips stemmed from my passion for Italian yachts. I'll talk much more about my boating interests in subsequent chapters, but here I'll mention that over the years, I bought four boats that were manufactured in Italy. One of them was custom built for me in Italy. I especially love Northern Italy, the Tuscany area.

Over the past several decades, I've purchased numerous European cars in America, then taken the car through European delivery. These vehicles have been mostly Mercedes, Porsche, or BMW. Those companies let you take delivery at their European factory. You can drive away from the factory in your new car, tour Europe in it, and when you're done driving around, you give the car back to the destination for shipment to the U.S. They ship it free of charge back to America. For the last twenty years or so, Mercedes has given customers a 10% discount if they buy a Mercedes on a "visiting program" such as this. I believe it's a tax issue, that doing business this way provides a tax benefit for the auto company. If you get a 10% discount on a car like that, it sometimes pays for the trip, or at least goes a long way toward it.

I believe travel is important for everyone. If you have the means to travel, I encourage you to do so. When you travel and meet different people, you learn about the ways in which all of us are different and also the ways in which all people have some commonalities. Travel is educational, exciting, and gives you perspective on your own life. I highly recommend everyone travel, especially internationally, if you are able.

A PASSION FOR CARS

Cars have always been a hobby of mine. Diana currently drives an Aston Martin, and my cars are mostly BMW, Mercedes, or Porsche. I currently have a Porsche SUV. We also have a Bentley convertible.

Italian cars have to be driven fast once in a while; otherwise, they react differently. They're made to be driven fast. If you get an Italian car and you don't drive it fast, you're likely to have technical prob-lems later on.

I love to drive, and I especially love driving all over Europe, from country to country. I'll admit it: I love to drive fast, especially in Europe. In America, I stick to the speed limit.

The German autobahn is something else, a network of highways with no posted speed limit in many areas. They sure didn't have that when I was growing up in Germany, and we have nothing like it in the United States. The fastest I've gone on the autobahn is about 140 miles an hour. But everybody else goes fast, too. You don't even realize you're driving that fast, because everyone else is, too. If you drove too slowly, you'd know it!

These days in Germany, when you're learning to drive, you must take an additional class on how to use the autobahn. You learn to drive fast, but you also learn to drive cautiously, looking out for fast cars coming up from behind. You stay in the right lane and only use the left lane for passing. If you remain in the left lane too long, they can give you a ticket.

Once, I got a ticket for being in the left lane too long. This was actually in Austria. I was only in the left lane for five minutes. There was a motorcycle behind me, and I told my girlfriend at the time, who was in the passenger seat, "I want to get out of the way for the motorcycle. I want to go a little faster, so I can get out of the traffic zone here." But I took too long doing that, apparently. The officer who stopped me spoke no English. But he gave me a ticket anyway, both for going too fast—Austria has a speed limit, and Germany does not—and for remaining in the left lane too long.

It was worth it, though. Every drive I've done through Europe has been well worth it.

WORK TOWARD YOUR LEISURE

In this chapter, I've talked about some pretty expensive hobbies. Obviously, I haven't had these expensive hobbies my entire adult life. When I was young and just getting started, I saved every penny I could. My first big indulgence was that 1946 Pontiac, and even that was reasonable, considering that it was a used car and I paid cash for it.

I will admit that these days, I have expensive tastes. But I worked my way up to them. I haven't always had that sort of interest. I've never gotten myself into debt for anything, especially a hobby. There's no reason to do that. I advise everyone to only pursue those hobbies that they can enjoy within the budget they have. Even if you're just getting started, there are plenty of things you can do for free: reading (the library is always free), dancing (once you learn, you can dance anywhere), and certainly spending time with friends and family.

As soon as your budget allows for it, I recommend setting aside a modest amount for hobbies and activities. It's important to be a well-rounded individual, and hobbies help with that.

Work hard, but don't work all the time. Find passions that you enjoy and that won't break the bank. As you work your way up, your hobbies and interests can change to reflect that.

CHALLENGE YOURSELF

•   What are your hobbies? How much time do you devote to hobbies and nonwork interests?

•   Do you like to read? What is your favorite genre? Do you ever read outside your favorite genre?

•   Do you like to travel? Where have you been? Where would you like to go?

•   If some of your interests and passions are currently beyond your means, what steps can you take toward a goal of being able to pursue these more expensive hobbies?

CHAPTER 13

ON THE WATER

STARTING "SMALL"

In the late 1960s, when my family was living in San Jose, our neighbors had a ski boat on a nearby lake. After they took us on their boat a few times, I said to Elke, "I'm going to the boat show in Los Angeles to buy a ski boat. It's a good way to get into boating on a small scale and see if we like it."

I took Susan with me, and we spent two days at the boat show.

We looked at every type of boat imaginable.

Other than the neighbors' ski boat, I hadn't spent much time on the water. But I *did* remember Mr. Edmond Cook's river barge on the Mississippi. Recalling that, I put aside the idea of a ski boat and decided to look at something a bit bigger.

I wound up buying a 32-foot Grand Banks, an ocean cruisingboat.

It was a Friday when I bought the boat. Having never been to sea before, I knew I'd need instructions on how to operate the boat. The salesman said, "I can show you on Monday. I'll show you how to take it into your boat slip and how to run the boat."

I called Elke, telling her to bring the other two girls down. I said, "We're going to take the boat from Newport Beach to Dana Point, and I want the whole family to be there."

That was the start of a hobby that lasted decades and provided countless hours of precious family time. Even now, Susan recalls, "During those years, my dad just kept getting busier and busier with his work, so he was becoming more distant from the family. But the magical ingredient that held our family together was the boat."

She's right. Suddenly, we had something we could all do together, something we all loved.

I spent the weekend reading everything I could about boating. By the time Elke, Veronica, and Lisa arrived, I felt confident that, combined with the salesman's instructions, I'd know enough about boating that I could manage to cruise from Newport Beach to Dana Point. It was a relatively short trip of about twenty nautical miles, a good first outing.

On Monday, the boat was launched, and we revved up the motor. It was a single-engine boat, not a twin engine. We motored to Dana Point without incident and stayed overnight.

The next day, we went to Catalina Island. This was a trip of about forty nautical miles—twice the distance, and into the open ocean. As we cruised along, I was quite proud of myself. I thought I was doing a great job, especially for only my second day operating a boat.

Then, suddenly, there was a big cruising ship coming toward us, a navy destroyer. Using light signals, they sent me Morse code. But I couldn't read Morse code and didn't know what they were telling me. It was later, after I'd learned Morse code—which I did, and fast— that I realized that what they were trying to tell me was, "Stay clear

of our wake."

That destroyer's wake was about ten feet high. When we hit that wake on our 32-foot Grand Banks, the bow actually dropped into the water. We were lucky to get out of that incident unscathed. I learned my lesson really fast, and I never did that again!

UP THE COAST

I traveled back and forth several more times from San Jose to the boat, docked in Newport Beach. Usually, I brought the family with me for weekend outings. I also continued to read everything I could about boating. My goal was to eventually take the boat all the way up the coast to San Francisco.

I learned there were a few tricky spots. For example, at Point Conception, just north of Santa Barbara, the current changes and can be troublesome. A lot of boats have capsized there. But I wanted to try it anyway.

When it was time to begin the big trip north, I said to Elke, "Tomorrow, we're leaving at four o'clock in the morning. Our first stop will be Santa Barbara." We had to leave Newport Beach at 4:00 AM to get into Santa Barbara before the winds picked up in the afternoon.

I'd read in my boating books that you never want to go *into* a marina at dark. You can *leave* at dark, but don't go in at dark, because too many lights can get you confused about where the harbor entrance is. So, we set a 4:00 AM departure time, with the goal of being in Santa Barbara at 3:00 in the afternoon.

We made it into Santa Barbara with no incident. The plan was that the next day, we'd cruise to San Simeon, up the coast. To do that, we'd have to go past Point Arguello and Point Conception.

I said, "I better double-check. There's a coast guard station here in Santa Barbara harbor. I'm going to ask them."

At the coast guard station, I said, "Can you give me some advice about the trouble everybody's been having at Point Conception and Point Arguello?"

The coast guard officer said, "We don't give advice, but the fishermen are right out there. They can tell you what you want to know."

I stopped at a fisherman's boat and made the same inquiry. "Yeah, we go fishing out there every day," he said.

"What's the deal about it being so dangerous?" I asked.

"Well, let me ask you," he replied. "What kind of boat do you have?"

I told him I had a 32-foot Grand Banks.

"You have a lot of glass," he said. "First thing you want to do is go to the hardware store, get some plywood, and nail it over the windows, so the waves won't blow out the glass."

I thanked him but didn't take his advice. It didn't seem logical to me.

The next morning, we left at four o'clock again. Grand Banks cruisers are very slow, with a top speed of about six knots. That's why we had to leave so early.

We had radar, which helped prevent me from hitting other boats or land in those dark, predawn hours. When we left Santa Barbara, Elke and the kids were sleeping, so it was only me running the boat. They didn't even know we were leaving.

About halfway to Point Conception, I saw lightning on the horizon, looking toward Point Arguello and Point Conception. I said to myself, "This doesn't look good. We're going back."

One conventional piece of boating wisdom is, "Don't take a chance." It's like piloting a small plane. You don't take a chance when the weather is bad.

I turned back, and by eight o'clock in the morning, we were back in our slip. The kids woke up and asked, "Are we there?"

"No, we're not there," I said. "We're in Santa Barbara again."

The next morning, we tried it again. We wanted to make sure we hit Point Arguello (the northern of the two points) at daylight, before the winds picked up. The smoothest water on the Southern California coastline is when the sun rises.

This time, we made it past Point Conception and Point Arguello. I'm pretty sure that if I'd ignored the "Don't take a chance" advice, the fisherman's advice to board up my windows would have been valid. But it might not have mattered, because the boat might have capsized anyway.

We made it to San Simeon, stayed there overnight, then went on to the next marina and the next, all the way up the coast: Monterey, Santa Cruz, and others. We always left in the dark to make sure we got into the next marina before three in the afternoon. We landed in Sausalito a week later.

There's an area called the Potato Patch Shoal at the mouth of the San Francisco Bay. A shallow reef of several square miles, it's an extremely rough area of water. The Potato Patch was named for the potato farms north of San Francisco, which during the 1800s would ship their products to San Francisco. It was not unusual for a potato boat to capsize on the sand bar and spill its load.

I did my studying on that, how to watch out for the Potato Patch. You must make sure you don't cut it too short. You want to come straight from the ocean. If you're too close to the shoreline, the waves break differently and get bigger. You've got to go in through the channel and be precise about it. I did that without incident that first time, on my way to Sausalito. And I did it without incident each additional time we cruised in that area.

Back in Newport Beach, the salesman who had sold me the boat came into the marina. He said to everyone, "I can't find Peter. Where is he? I need to show him how to run the boat."

"Oh," they told him. "Peter left with his wife and kids to go up the coast to San Francisco."

"Oh, my God," he said. "He's going to kill himself."

But I didn't kill myself or anybody else. I had no sea boating experience before buying the 32-foot Grand Banks. No deep-sea experience, no ocean experience. But I did my homework. I read every book I could about it. I called and wrote letters to people who had similar boats to mine, asking, "Can you tell me what I need to do if I want to go up the coast?"

They gave me ample advice, for which I was grateful. I studied to a T how to run the boat up and down the coast. Because I took the time to study it beforehand, my family and I were able to make our way north without incident.

Just as in business, if you're going to try out a hobby that's new to you—especially one like boating, where there's danger involved if you make a mistake—it's vital to be thorough in your research. It's also helpful to reach out to others who have more experience than you do. This isn't the time to be cocky. It's the time to read, question, listen, and learn, and always, always, put safety at the forefront.

A FAMILY AFFAIR

As Susan mentioned earlier, the boat really drew our family together. She recalls, "Everybody had to clean the boat. It was in a slip, and there was always dust. Windows had to be cleaned. Even though my sisters were challenged, we all cleaned the boat."

Susan was 10 years old when I purchased my first boat, and she gave a lot of hands-on help. Together, she and I sanded and varnished the teak rails. She says, "For me, it was a magical time, because my dad was teaching me a craft that he knew—and we were together."

I enjoyed that, too. I loved being present for those moments, because not only was it family time, it was family time with purpose. The boat caused me to be present. On the water, you have to be present, or you screw up. It's as simple as that.

Susan goes on, "My dad and I did all the navigating on the boat. He would figure out the weather, currents, and tides, and plan how the trip would best play out to arrive at known treacherous areas at the calmest times. We had very little navigation equipment. There was no GPS in those days, only paper charts and radar to show us approaching weather. My dad always tracked where we were on the chart, calculating our distance by the slow pace of the diesel engine. It was scary, adventuresome, calm, beautiful, and best of all, it was time with my dad."

TIME FOR AN UPGRADE

After we landed in Sausalito, I kept the boat docked there. But I joined the St. Francis Yacht Club across the bay in San Francisco, because I wanted to learn from the club's members. We did a lot of ocean cruising on the Grand Banks 32, but we also cruised inland, in the Sacramento Delta.

The Sacramento Delta is an inland river delta and estuary that stretches from San Francisco Bay to the Central Valley. On the eastern edge, the Delta forms at the confluence of the Sacramento and San Joaquin rivers; the water flows westward to the bay, then into the Pacific Ocean. Including land and water, the Sacramento Delta covers about 1,100 miles of waterways.

The St. Francis Yacht Club had an island on the Sacramento Delta called Tinsley Island. We could go there as members and tie up for a weekend, then return to San Francisco to go back to work the next day. That was a great benefit of belonging to the St. Francis Yacht Club.

After a few years, I decided that we needed a bigger boat. The Grand Banks 32 only had a forward berth that slept two. Other passengers (in our case, the kids) had to sleep in the galley, where the table turned into a bed.

I went to the boat show again and bought a 36-foot Grand Banks. It had both forward and aft staterooms, with a living room in the middle. I kept the Grand Banks 36 for four or five years, doing that same trip up and down the coast, as well as cruising in the Sacramento Delta.

MEXICAN CRUISING

Again, after several years I decided I wanted to trade up. This time, I bought a 48-foot Hatteras trawler. I bought it in Florida, taking delivery in Fort Lauderdale. From there, I took it down the waterway to Miami. Because I didn't know the local waters and didn't have time to learn them, I had a local guide with me, as well as a captain to help me get acquainted with the boat.

After that, I flew back to California. At that time, I had a lot of new projects in development. I couldn't take the time off from work to pilot the Hatteras all the way back to California. So, the captain I hired brought the boat through the Panama Canal and up the Mexican coastline to San Diego. In San Diego, I took over. By myself, I took the boat from San Diego to Newport Beach, where I had a slip.

In the Hatteras 48, I made about five trips down to Mexico. I did those back and forth without a crew or a captain, but I did often take a buddy or two along. From San Diego to Cabo San Lucas, it took two days and nights nonstop, with no marina in between for supplies or resting. We stayed twenty to thirty miles offshore to be safe from running aground.

By this time, the late 1970s, my kids were older and weren't as into boating anymore. I was married to Angela, and sometimes she came along, but often it was just me and a few other fellows.

With my buddies, we'd cruise all night long. We cruised nonstop from San Diego to Cabo San Lucas. That trip took three nights and four days, going down without stopping. The boat had enough fuel to make that trip.

We took turns being on watch. Everything was on radar, and we stayed about twenty miles offshore, so there was no chance of running aground unless something malfunctioned with the steering.

One time, I was down in Cabo with the boat and ready to bring it back. Two friends of mine were going to help me cruise up the coast. Going up the coast is harder than going down the coast; it's like you're going uphill. You're going up into the waves, and it can be treacherous.

One buddy backed out. It's better to have a crew of three than two, so we asked around at the harbor. We learned about a young kid who wanted a ride up the coast.

"He doesn't need money," we were told. "He just wants a ride up.

He'll help you with the boat."

We looked him over, and my buddy, Dave Ralstin, said, "That kid looks like he's on drugs."

I said, "Well, we'll just take the boat alone up the coast. Just the two of us."

"How are we going to do that, Peter?" Dave asked.

"Very simple," I replied. "We do four hours on and four hours off. You take a four-hour shift, and I take four hours sleeping. Then I take a four-hour shift, and you sleep. And so on."

When we left Cabo San Lucas, several other boats were leaving at the same time. We had other boats on radar that were probably between five and ten miles from us. We kept in radio communication with them, which gave us a comfort level of not being out there alone.

Still, the water was rough that day. We got a call from the captain of an 85-foot fishing boat. He said, "We're going to anchor. There's an island there—the Cedros Island, an uninhabited island where we can anchor. You can come over and have dinner with us tonight if you anchor there, too."

"Fine," I said. "We'll do that."

We anchored the Hatteras about a hundred feet from them. We climbed into a rubber life raft. In a rubber life raft, you've got to be very careful. I had just read a story about life rafts drifting out to sea from the wind. The people in them were never found.

I said to Dave, "We've got to be careful. But there's no wind, so let's go."

We made it to the fishing boat with no incident. There were about four or five fishermen on it, and they had a chef on board. We had a nice time with them, but eventually, around 9:30, it was time to go back to my boat.

Unfortunately, the wind had picked up and was running about ten to fifteen miles an hour. I said to my buddy, "We're not going with this wind."

Safety: rule number one!

We stayed another hour on the fishing boat, and after the wind died down, we got into our rubber life raft and ferried back to my boat before the wind picked up again. After we made it back to the Hatteras, we headed north again, staying fifteen or twenty miles offshore.

We weren't home free yet, however. The sea was rough on that journey. During one of my four-hour sleeping shifts, the pilot seat on the bridge jumped out of its socket and was rocking back and forth. Dave climbed up to secure it, not a good thing to do. He could have been thrown overboard. He was terrified!

The Hatteras had a leak in the fuel tank. The fuel tank was in the bilge, and every three hours or so the engine shut down, because there was water in the fuel. The only one who could change the fuel filters was me. I had it down to a science. I went down, and within a minute or less, I had that filter changed and the boat running again.

That trip was quite an experience. When we finally reached San Diego, we almost keeled over from exhaustion.

Did I fear for my life on that trip? Absolutely. Dave, too, was terrified. At one point, he used ship-to-shore radio to propose to his girlfriend, Kathy, telling her, "I want to marry you when I get back." I guess he figured that if he didn't make it home, he wanted her to know that he'd hoped to be her husband.

I kept the Hatteras 48 at Newport Beach. I did about ten trips to the San Francisco Bay and back on that boat. Many of those trips blend together in my memory, but I'll never forget the Mexico trips, especially the one Dave and I took!

BIGGER AND FASTER

The thing about cruising boats is, they're kind of addictive. And once you have one, you start thinking about an upgrade. At least, I did.

So, after a few years of owning the Hatteras 48, I bought a new boat in Florida again, a 58-foot Hatteras. It was a beautiful cruising boat with three bedrooms, two bathrooms, and two powerful engines.

The Hatteras 58 could go fifteen knots, which was a big improve-ment over the Hatteras 48—and certainly a huge jump from the six-knot top speed of my first boat, the Grand Banks 32!

I kept the Hatteras 58 in Newport Beach, at the Balboa Bay Club. We cruised on that boat many a time up and down the coast. Then I kept it up in Sausalito for a while, and again did a lot of cruising in the Sacramento Delta.

During this time, I was married to Angela. In 1984, she decided to throw a fiftieth birthday party for me on the boat. We started the party at four in the afternoon, with about twenty-five people on the boat. Mostly it was our friends, but my daughter, Susan, was there, too, pregnant at the time with her first child.

The boat was loaded with people, but I had life vests on board for everybody. As I've said, I knew and respected the need for safety first.

Everyone wanted to go for a cruise. So out we went, cruising in San Francisco Bay. We didn't stop anywhere; we just cruised around

for an hour. The lights of the city were on, and it was beautiful.

I kept thinking what an amazing thing it was, to be spending my fiftieth birthday this way. Doing something like that, cruising San Francisco Bay on a boat that size and entertaining twenty-five people on it, was something my younger self never would have imagined.

When we got back to Sausalito, it was very dark, and I had a little trouble finding the buoys in the bay that keep you from hitting the rocks. But I knew enough about the bay by this time that I knew my way, even without the buoys. I used radar to locate the buoys, land objects, and harbor entrances. We made it to the marina without incident, and I happily said goodbye to my guests and thanked them for spending my birthday with me. In return, they thanked Angela and me for a great evening on the water.

WORK YOUR WAY UP

All the boating experiences I've described here are examples of how you have to work your way up. Yes, some people start out with wealth, but even if you weren't born rich, like I wasn't, you can start small and work up. That's what I did, both in business and in enjoying hobbies such as boating.

True, the Grand Banks 32 was more than I'd planned on when I went to my first boat show. But I could afford that boat, and I studied carefully how to operate it safely. If either of those things had been untrue—if I couldn't afford it or didn't feel I could keep myself safe and ensure the safety of everyone on board and around me in the water—then I wouldn't have bought the boat.

The two Grand Banks boats and the two Hatteras boats were my first forays into boating. I greatly enjoyed my time on each of those boats when I owned them. But with each of them, when it was time to upgrade, I knew it.

After I'd owned the Hatteras 58 for a few years, I knew that time had come again. I was ready for something really fast and, eventually, really big.

CHALLENGE YOURSELF

- Have you ever had a hobby lead to learning a new skill? What was the learning curve like?

- Do you share hobbies with your family and loved ones? A hobby that takes too much time away from those we care about can be detrimental to relationships. If your hobbies are taking you away from others, how could you combine your interests with your relationships?

- If your hobbies have you dreaming about large-ticket items, what steps can you take to make those dreams into reality without going into debt for it?

CHAPTER 14

TRADING UP

"IT'S REALLY FAST"

In the mid-1980s, Angela and I went to the boat show in Florida and spent quite a bit of time looking at Italian boats. The workmanship was impeccable, like nothing in the United States.

An Italian boat that particularly caught my eye was a 50-foot Riva. "It's really fast," the salesman said. "About twenty-eight knots."

For the non-boaters reading this, that's about thirty-two miles an hour. I know that doesn't sound very fast, and if you're on land, it

isn't. But on the water, it's lightning speed.

"Holy smokes, that's fast," I said. "Let's buy it."

We bought the Riva 50, but we hadn't sold the Hatteras 58 yet. For a while, we had two boats. We kept both of them in Newport Beach.

As I'm sure you've guessed by now, I love a good entrepreneurial story. Riva goes back all the way to 1842, when its founder, Pietro Riva, began designing and building fishing boats following a sudden storm on Lake Iseo, Italy, that decimated the local fishing fleet. Using his profits from the sale of the fishing boats, Pietro Riva opened a shipping yard, where he created custom-designed, beautiful, classy wooden boats. Over the years, Riva's family business grew and expanded from service and working boats to recreational craft. By the time I bought my first Riva, they were producing a wide, diverse fleet, including fiberglass speedboats like my Riva 50.

We went cruising many times on the Riva 50. I loved the speed of that boat, but it was smaller than my Hatteras. What I really wanted was a 58-foot Riva. This boat was new on the market, and it was astonishing in its speed, grace, and beauty.

I decided to call the Riva factory. I knew the man who ran it. My idea was to see if I could become a dealer for Riva on the west coast of the United States. Then I could buy more boats—and make a profit at it.

The factory manager said, "Well, Mr. Paulsen, I'd say yes, except that we have a very important man from Seattle who also wants to be our dealer on the West Coast."

"Hmm, I know an important man in Seattle who's into boating," I said. "That can't be anybody else but my friend Craig McCaw."

That's exactly who it was. Craig McCaw was the owner of Cellular One, which he eventually sold to AT&T for $12 billion. I'd known Craig for many years. Before he moved to Seattle, he'd lived in Santa Barbara when I lived near there, in Montecito.

How we got to be friends is a good story. I'd met Craig a few times in Santa Barbara, but I didn't really know him. Then one time, Angela and I were in Seattle, and we picked up a copy of the *Forbes* book about the wealthiest people in the world. Craig was in it, and so was Orin Edson, another boating man, the owner of Bayliner Boats. As we were paging through it, I said to Angela, "Look at these two people; we know them. Craig McCaw and Orin Edson. They're both from Seattle, and they're both billionaires. Let's give them a call and see if they want to go to dinner with us."

I'd met Orin Edson only once. But I called him and said, "This is Peter Paulsen. We've met once or twice, and I'm in Seattle with my wife. We'd love to have dinner with you."

"Yeah, that'll be fine," he said. He named a restaurant, and we agreed on a time.

Then I called Craig McCaw and said, "Craig, we're having dinner with Orin Edson. You probably know him. How would you like to come to dinner with us?"

"Sounds good, Peter," he said. "We'll meet you for dinner."

It was a very big dinner bill. They were two billionaires, and in relation to them, I was nobody. But I invited them, so I paid for everyone's dinner.

I was just a normal American guy. I had a good income, but I was definitely not in their league financially. Nonetheless, I called a couple of billionaires and invited them to dinner.

Sometimes, you have to stick your neck out and just see what happens. I figured the worst that would happen is that they'd say no. But they accepted my invitation, and we became friends after that. Later, I connected more with both of them. Edson even invited me for a ride in his private helicopter.

After talking to the Riva factory manager, I called Craig McCaw

and asked, "What are you doing with Riva? I want to be their West Coast dealer, too, because I want a bigger Riva." I went on, "Why don't we split the territory? You take the northern area, Seattle, where you live. I'll take the southern area."

He said, "That sounds like a good idea. Let's start a corporation." I declined that offer and suggested we have separate companies. "That way, you can do things your way and I'll do them my way," I

said. And that's what we did.

I became a dealer for Riva, and I got my Riva 58. But I only sold two boats, one to myself, and one to someone else.

I realized my heart wasn't in making money on boats. As a dealer, I felt like I was missing the fun of boat ownership. It made boating feel like work instead of play. And I already had plenty of other work.

This was another lesson in knowing what you want. I wanted that Riva 58, and I figured out a great way to get it—and get into a new line of business at the same time. But when I realized that the Riva dealership wasn't for me, I got out.

MAKING TIME FOR FUN

I didn't always have time to get away. I was heavily involved in business at the time, with my building projects and my bank, and I couldn't take a lot of time off. So, we kept our boat in Newport Beach and did one week at a time cruising.

In addition to cruising on our own boats, sometimes we were invited to go cruising in other areas with some of my billionaire friends. I've cruised on vessels between 100 feet and 150 feet in length, in areas as diverse as Panama, Australia, and Tahiti. We cruised in the West Indian Islands and off the coast of Cuba. On these trips, I was invited as a guest. Sometimes I think that's the better way to go cruising. It's certainly less of a commitment!

When I bought the 58-foot Riva, I was still married to Angela. We had that boat for many years. We still went to the boat show every year in Florida, but we also started to go to the boat show in Italy. It was there that I met boating people from Riva, as well as another Italian boat maker, Ferretti.

Unlike Riva, Ferretti is a relatively new player in the Italian boat market. The company was founded in 1968 by two brothers, Norberto and Alessandro Ferretti. They began by selling boats manufactured by other companies, but in 1971, they designed and produced their first boat, a sailboat. Soon, they shifted to designing and manufacturing motor yachts. Their first model debuted in 1982, and they've expanded their line ever since. Ironically, they even eventually acquired Riva, which they bought in 2000.

I fell in love with Ferretti's products and decided to buy a 70-foot Ferretti. The Ferretti 70 was a wonderful boat, but after a few years, I decided it was too small.

Indeed, this hobby is addictive!

GODDESS OF BEAUTY AND LOVE

I wanted an 80-foot Ferretti, but the boat I wanted was not built yet. I told the Ferretti dealer, "I'm going to buy the boat in Italy and soon as it's built, I want it shipped to Florida. I'll take it from there." The fact that the boat was not built yet worked in my favor, because it gave me the opportunity to request some modifications. By this time, it was the late 1990s, and marine technology had come a long way since Susan and I studied paper navigation charts aboard our Grand Banks 32. I wanted all the latest technology on my Ferretti

80. I requested double GPS screens in the panel house, which meant I'd have a backup screen in case one failed. The two screens also allowed me to plan. I used one for long trips, for reaching out twenty to thirty miles, and the other for reaching two to five miles out. Either way, I knew what was going on around me.

I had my Ferretti 80 equipped with bow thrusters and stern thrusters, so I could move the boat sideways within the marina complex. There were controls on the aft deck and on top, so I could control it from any direction I wanted to go. It made boat handling easier, even when I did it solo—which I always did, other than a deck hand who managed the lines when we tied up to a dock.

Another conversion I requested was to have one of the four standard staterooms turned into an office. This allowed me to work while on board the boat. I had my office outfitted with state-of-the-art equipment and technology, allowing me to stay in touch with those on shore with whom I needed to conduct business. The office was so advanced that in 2001, a publication called the *Yacht Owner's Guide* did a two-page spread on the *Freya* and me, much of it explaining the technology and communications in my onboard office.

The Ferretti 80 took a year to build. When it was done, it was shipped from Italy to Florida. I christened it the *Freya*, after the Norse goddess of beauty and love. I took delivery in Florida, and again I had my boat captained through the Panama Canal and delivered to San Diego. From there, I took over.

I made many a trip on the *Freya* to Mexico. I went to Puerto Vallarta and Cabo San Lucas. I loved cruising the coast of Mexico in the wintertime on the *Freya*, because it was beautiful and warm there, and cruising those picturesque waters on that wonderful boat was a joy. That was the most fantastic boat I ever had.

Eventually, I brought the *Freya* up to Bellingham, Washington.

By this time, I had a home there, sort of a gentleman's farm.

In the next chapter, I'll tell you all about a fantastic hotel on the water in Bellingham. For now, suffice to say I docked the *Freya* at that particular hotel. I kept my boat in front of the hotel for a while, and later I had a beautiful, 85-foot boathouse built for it in Vancouver.

The waterways around Vancouver are gorgeous, so I wanted to keep the boat there. We'd cruise on the *Freya* to the San Juan Islands and up the coast, up into waterways halfway to Alaska. Cruising Canadian waterways is like cruising the fjords of Norway. The scenery is spectacular, and there are coves where you can anchor and enjoy the view. These are protected waterways, hundreds and hundreds of miles without being exposed to the open ocean. We went to Desolation Sound and all the beautiful, picturesque areas around there. In the summer, the water in Desolation Sound is seventy-five degrees. Waterfalls are right beside your boat when you anchor down in that area. It's incredible cruising ground up there.

We also liked going into Victoria, British Columbia, docking up, and enjoying afternoon tea at the Empress Hotel. Victoria is a city that's reminiscent of European cities, and going there felt very European to me.

Additionally, we sometimes took the *Freya* south, going into the San Francisco Bay. One time, everybody was on top of the bridge, on the front of the boat. We were moving slowly, about fourteen knots. The waves were breaking about three or four miles offshore. That meant huge swells, probably a hundred feet long, were coming in, breaking way before they hit the beach.

I said, "Uh-uh, that's danger."

We had to go right into the channel, making sure not to shortcut the entrance to the San Francisco Bay. If we didn't go straight into the channel, we would have had the waves going over the top of the boat. That's another thing I learned to be safe about.

Susan also has a story about the *Freya*. She says, "I met my second husband, Rick, in 1992, and in 2000, we got married on the back of the *Freya*. We put the wedding together in two weeks. I didn't want or need a big, frou-frou wedding. My dad mentioned he was going to be in San Francisco with the boat, so we asked him if we could get married on it and he said of course we could. We had to find an officiant, but everyone we wanted to invite was close by and able to join us on the boat." She goes on, "Like everything my dad does, it unfolded into a perfect day, including the weather."

THE END OF AN ERA

You might think that by the time I owned the *Freya*, I hired other people to do all the maintenance on my boat. After all, it was a big boat and I was, by this time, in my seventies.

But you'd be wrong about that. I still loved working on my boat, every bit as much as I'd loved it with my very first boat, the Grand Banks 32. Susan says, "Even as recently as 2011, Dad would do small refinishing projects on the teak wood on board the *Freya*. You could tell it gave him a sense of accomplishment to enhance it himself."

For the past couple of years, I haven't been able to use the *Freya*, due to the pandemic preventing travel from the U.S. to Canada. So when somebody wanted to buy it, I said, "Go ahead and take it. I can't even get to the boat."

It was the end of an era. But it was an era about which I don't regret a single second.

ANOTHER BOAT SOMEDAY?

Often, I'm asked this question. I'll admit I think about it. If I bought another boat, I'd probably store it in San Diego. But I'm not sure I'll ever buy another one.

You can also charter big boats, which is something Diana and I are considering for future boating trips. I've loved every minute of being a boat owner, but it's a lot of responsibility. At this stage of my life, chartering is easier. This way, we can have whatever boat we want.

The sky (or the water) is the limit!

CHALLENGE YOURSELF

- Think about the hobbies and interests you've had over the years. Have they changed or remained the same?

- What does the phrase "stick your neck out" mean to you? Are you willing to take risks that people might reject you or criticize you? If this worries you, what steps can you take to feel more confident asking for what you want?

- What is your biggest dream? What are you doing to work toward it?

CHAPTER 15
A HOBBY INSPIRES A NEW PROJECT

WHAT THIS TOWN NEEDS

As mentioned in the last chapter, by the late 1990s, I was doing a lot of boating around Bellingham, Washington and storing the *Freya* there. My relaxation and vacation

time was mostly spent on the water, and I very much enjoyed cruising in the waterways of the Pacific Northwest.

Because I was spending so much time in Bellingham, I noticed there were no hotels on the water. Other than on their boats (if they had a boat), there was nowhere on the water for people to stay. Like many others, when I was there, I stayed in the only nearby hotel, which was a Best Western.

Curious, I asked other hotel guests why they were staying there. "We looked for a place on the water, but there *is* no place on the

water," they said. "The Best Western is the finest hotel in Bellingham."

Such a beautiful town and stunning waterfront, and the "finest hotel" was a Best Western? Nothing against Best Western, but I thought Bellingham deserved something more special than that.

Eventually, I decided to buy a home in Bellingham. I ended up with a 68-acre "gentleman's farm." It had no animals, other than a couple of alpacas. I liked the setting. It had a view of Mt. Baker, a snowcapped mountain right outside the window. It was a great getaway.

That solved my own dilemma about accommodations in Bellingham, but I continued to think about what people had said: that there was nowhere on the water to stay. I decided Bellingham needed a luxury hotel on the water.

THIS SPOT WILL DO NICELY

I noticed there was a parcel of land on the end of a peninsula, about twenty acres, very industrialized and clearly underutilized. There was nothing on it but one restaurant. The views were stunning, and I could visualize a gorgeous hotel there. I decided to contact the Port of Bellingham to inquire about buying and developing the land.

The Port of Bellingham is a Washington State special purpose government. The Port manages all the public land in Whatcom County, including all tenants of the Port (around 250 currently), the Bellingham International Airport, two marinas, and several industrial parks. The Port owns and operates the Bellingham Cruise Terminal, which houses the Alaska Marine Highway System, as well as an Amtrak station.

According to Shirley McFearin, the Port of Bellingham's Director of Real Estate, "The Port of Bellingham is governed by a nonpartisan port commission composed of three elected officials. They provide policy direction, but they also vote on real estate transactions for the Port. Everything goes in front of the port commission in an open, public meeting. The public can voice concerns or make comments about a project. The Port of Bellingham is the largest landholder in Whatcom County, and all of their property is in the public trust."

Including that twenty-acre parcel that I thought would be perfect for a waterfront hotel.

Shirley, who has managed the Port's real estate portfolio for the past thirty-five years, remembers the first time she and I met. "One day in 1997," she says, "Mr. Paulsen walked into the Port offices, approached the reception desk and said, 'I want to build a waterfront hotel on your land.' The receptionist called me and said there was a man in the lobby who wanted to build a hotel. I get those kinds of inquiries all the time, and I do try to give people my time and attention, so I said to send him in. When I greeted Mr. Paulsen, I noticed that he was super high energy, completely amped up and excited.

"He came into my office, and we chatted for maybe thirty minutes. Well, *we* didn't—*he* did. He went on and on about how we needed a luxury hotel on the waterfront. I was thinking good grief, who *is* this guy?

"After that, he came by every few weeks. After the first time, he never stopped at the reception desk. He'd say, 'I'm going to Shirley's office,' and just walk right by like he owned the Port of Bellingham. He'd walk into my office, sit at my table, and ask for a cup of Earl Grey tea. He used to take a ton of vitamins, and I'd watch him and think, good grief, no wonder you're so amped up, with all of these vitamins you take. He'd always tell me, 'You've got to take your vitamins to keep your energy up.'

"Mr. Paulsen is very charismatic, with an incredible heart," Shirley says. "He has a big heart for Bellingham. He's a generous, kind man. But when I first met him, I wasn't too sure. I admit that."

INITIAL IDEAS

The first thing I learned from Shirley was that the land I was interested in wasn't for sale. Because the land is in the public trust, the Port only leases it. It doesn't sell the land.

"But I want to buy it," I said.

"I'm sorry, Mr. Paulsen," Shirley replied. "It's not for sale. But it can be leased."

"Okay, that's fine," I agreed. "We can negotiate a lease."

I asked Shirley to walk the property with me. I said, "You need a hotel back here. You need office buildings here, and apartments." I told her she needed to get the trees and bushes cleaned up. I said the grasses were too high. I told her, "You've got to get this place cleaned up. I'm building a hotel here."

"Well, Mr. Paulsen," Shirley said. "I need to see a proposal. I need to understand what you want to do."

"I know what I want to do," I said. "I want to build a luxury hotel. And you guys are just going to love it."

Shirley told me that ten or fifteen years earlier, the Marriott corporation had wanted to build a fifteen-story hotel on that site. The project was turned down by the community because the community didn't want a big hotel there.

I said, "Well, I can do something on a smaller scale."

I spent $20,000 to develop a plan for a hotel and office building. It included the concept and layouts. My idea was to build a European, boutique-style hotel.

Shirley explains, "Mr. Paulsen did scale back. I think he originally was thinking something like 150 rooms. But when I told him what happened with Marriott, he decided to do more of a boutique hotel.

That's what the Port wanted to see out there—something that was fantastic but not overbuilt."

Shirley and I also negotiated what the rent structure would look like. We ended up agreeing on an 80-year lease. I would have preferred to buy the land, but I was comfortable with eighty years leasing it. I figured I wasn't going to keep the hotel that long anyway.

Once I had my proposal together, Shirley took it to the Port commission in a closed session, not open to the public. It was a staff presentation; it was Shirley explaining to the Port commission what I wanted to do.

Shirley says, "Having been here for so many years, I have a pretty good read of the Port commission. I came out of that meeting knowing that, yeah, we wanted a hotel out there. But it had to make economic sense for the taxpayers of Whatcom County, and it had to be a nice hotel. I felt confident Mr. Paulsen could deliver that."

I felt confident, too. That said, whenever I started a new project and I wasn't sure how it would turn out, I liked to have a backup plan. For the hotel, my backup plan was an assisted living facility. I ran the numbers, knowing it would work, also.

It's always a good idea to have a backup plan. But I hoped I wouldn't need to use it. I really wanted to build a hotel!

HOTEL DESIGN

Like all my other businesses, before I became a hotel owner, I had no hotel experience. I still had the shopping centers in Phoenix, but I'd sold one of my office complexes. I didn't need money for a loan because I financed the hotel myself, out of cash flow from the sale of my bank.

I made it a point to become knowledgeable in the hotel business. Everywhere I stayed, I asked questions and observed what that hotel was up to, how it was being operated. I'd been doing this for years anyway because I found the hotel industry intriguing, particularly in Europe. I liked the class and style of European hotels.

In each hotel I visited, I talked with managers as well as other employees. I also talked with hotel guests to see what they liked.

I decided to build a hotel that reflected what I would want to experience as a guest in a hotel. I asked myself, *when I stay in a hotel, what do I like to see? What do I wish I saw more of?*

I like tasteful, well-appointed hotel rooms. I enjoy a fireplace in the room. I want a bathroom with the tub and shower stall separate from each other, rather than a shower within the tub. I want granite countertops. I want well-insulated, soundproofed walls, so I can't hear the neighbors next door.

Spacious rooms are appealing, so instead of typical hotel rooms, I designed suites. Each suite would feature a sitting area, a bedroom area with a king-sized bed and TV, and a big sliding window overlooking the harbor and marina.

Something I've observed over the years is that in hotels that have adjoining rooms where one door opens to the next room for people to share, even when the doors are closed, you can always hear noise through the doors. Instead, I developed a floor plan with an interior foyer that was shared by two suites. You'd go into the entry foyer, then from there into each suite. In my hotels, to have a shared space between two suites, you'd close the outside door of the entry foyer and leave both suite doors open. This is a much quieter design than the typical door-in-the-wall that connects two rooms in many hotels.

Another feature I want in a hotel is an upscale restaurant. I want to enjoy cocktail hour and delicious dinners. I also want different sizes and styles of meeting spaces, to accommodate varied event needs.

While doing all this research, I read somewhere that people love staying in a lighthouse. It's very romantic (depending on the lighthouse, of course). I decided I needed a lighthouse as part of the design, so I developed a lighthouse plan at the harbor entrance, on the hotel property. It would be situated about ten feet from the hotel, with a living room, kitchen, and bathroom on the first floor, a master suite on the second floor, and spiral staircase to an observation level, including a breakfast bar, 360 degrees of windows, and a wraparound terrace with outdoor seating.

All those ideas turned into my concepts for the 68-room (plus lighthouse) Hotel Bellwether.

Once I had my plans in place, I said to myself, *I really can't be that good at hotel design. I better check with a hotel consulting firm.*

I went to Seattle, to a consulting firm, and I showed them my ideas and floor plans. Then I said, "Tell me what I'm doing wrong." "The first thing you're doing wrong," they said, "is that you have every room with one king-sized bed. You need thirty percent double occupancy. You need thirty percent of the rooms to have two double beds."

I thought (but didn't say aloud), *the hell I do.*

My intention with the Hotel Bellwether was for it to be a romantic getaway, not a business hotel. And I didn't want it to be a hotel where people are packed into every available inch of space. So I nixed his idea and retained my design, my way.

NEGOTIATIONS

The Port and I spent a year negotiating the terms and conditions of the lease, and then the project went to a public hearing. Shirley presented the project to the commission and showed some renderings of what the hotel would look like. That meeting was open to the public.

Although the Port commission was in favor of someone tastefully developing that land, the general public in Bellingham did not care for the idea of a hotel coming in. Many residents didn't want any expansion whatsoever. It took a lot of convincing, but because of the boutique nature of the hotel and the tasteful design, I got my zoning for the hotel. It also helped that the city council, along with the Port

of Bellingham commission, liked my plans.

"The commission was very supportive," Shirley said. "They had already met Mr. Paulsen, and they really liked him. In the open public meeting, they approved the lease for him to build his hotel. It was a 3-0 vote. I remember that perfectly."

Unlike most of my projects, which I'd named myself, I didn't name the Hotel Bellwether. The Port hired a firm to work with us to come up with the name. The entire development is called Bellwether on the Bay. I like the name. It's memorable, and it fits Bellingham and the hotel.

As part of the project, the Port decided to build a parking garage underneath the hotel, as well as two office buildings. Their plan was to build a 40,000-square-foot, three-story office building, then a sister building of about 35,000 square feet.

I told Shirley that I wanted a private parking section for the hotel. I wanted it walled off, so the hotel guests would be able to park separately from the office building users. I told her I wanted a separate street entrance to the underground parking for the hotel. From there, people would be able to take an elevator right to the hotel lobby.

Shirley says, "Plans to build two office buildings and a 280-stall parking garage had been in the works anyway, before Mr. Paulsen came to us with his hotel idea. Once we learned that he wanted to build a hotel, our vision became two office buildings and Mr. Paulsen's hotel looking over the water.

"We went ahead and built our underground parking garage. Then, I remember negotiating with Mr. Paulsen. I said, 'You don't have to build a foundation now for your hotel, because we built the parking garage. But you have to pay me something for the deck.'

"'You were going to build it anyway,' Mr. Paulsen said. 'Why should I pay for something you were going to build anyway?'

"I didn't want to lose the deal, which I knew would spur huge development on that site for the Port. If we could secure the deal with Mr. Paulsen, it would change everything down there, for the better. So we let it go, and Mr. Paulsen got his foundation for free."

To me, this type of negotiation is just common sense. I didn't know if Shirley would push back or not, but I wasn't going to just cave in and pay for the foundation when I had the possibility of getting it for free. So I presented a reasonable argument, and the Port agreed.

Would I have walked away from the deal if the Port made me pay for the foundation? Maybe. But by then, I was truly enamored with the idea of the

Hotel Bellwether. I wouldn't have easily given it up.

I think it's always worth asking for what you want. You're not guaranteed to get it, but if you never ask, you'll never know.

A HOTEL AND AN OFFICE BUILDING GO UP

As with all my projects, I oversaw the construction. I used a local contractor, and the Port was very enthusiastic about that. As in most other cities, they love to see local contractors building facilities in Bellingham.

The hotel opened in 2000. It's top of the line, the best hotel in Whatcom County. The lighthouse is stunning and very popular. From the start, it was always in demand. Bellingham has a fireworks show on the bay every Fourth of July, and you couldn't ask for a more perfect spot for watching them.

Recently, Diana and I wanted to stay in the lighthouse, but it was booked solid. I don't own the Hotel Bellwether anymore, but even the builder and former owner must get in line, if he wants to stay in the lighthouse.

I also built a 250-foot dock for hotel guests to dock their boats. I made use of that myself quite a bit, and it's always been popular with hotel guests who also own boats.

There are also several charter-boat outfits in Bellingham, and they love the Hotel Bellwether. Their clients can stay in the hotel, do some shopping, and stock up on everything they need for their charter boat experience. One Bellingham charter boat company president was interviewed for an article in the spring of 2001, in a publication called *Home Port*. The article states: "The advantages of shopping in the uncongested, relaxing, and beautiful surroundings of Bellingham, paired with first class lodging, creates an optimal buying environment. He [the charter boat outfit president] credits the Hotel Bellwether with maximizing his customers' shopping experience."

Their lodging experiences are maximized, too. Inside the hotel, everything is fantastic. In the suites, the sitting areas are homelike, with reclining chairs for TV watching or relaxing, an antique hutch for hiding the TV, and tasteful artwork on the walls. And, of course, a fireplace in the corner of every room. Each bathroom features a Jacuzzi tub and a separate shower stall, just like I wanted. There are granite countertops and attractive tile on the bathroom floors and walls.

All this makes it a very livable situation, which in turn makes people want to stay longer, because they like it so much.

Once I built the hotel, I told Shirley that I wanted to build one of the office buildings that the Port had in the works.

"The Port's going to build the office buildings," she said. "I want to build one of them," I repeated.

She considered. "Here's what we want it to look like," she said, showing me the plans. "You can build it, but you have to build it to our specs, because we want it to be the sister building to the other Port building."

"Okay, no problem," I told her. "I can do that." And I did. Using

the Port's specs, I built one of the office buildings they'd been considering. It opened in 2003.

About that transaction, Shirley says, "Mr. Paulsen is a very tough negotiator. He wants what he wants."

She's right about that. And most of the time, I get it.

As I said—it never hurts to ask. If you ask for things rationally, present a reasonable argument, and are willing to listen to the other party's concerns, you often can get what you're after.

THEY LOVE IT!

The Hotel Bellwether turned out to be a fabulous draw. People flock to it for vacations, especially romantic getaways. It's also the perfect spot for a wedding.

Shirley says, "The hotel was very well received by the community. Partly because it's beautiful, but also, I think, because of how admired Mr. Paulsen was in Bellingham."

The hotel has a restaurant right on the water. There are beautiful views, and it's a great place to have lunch or dinner, or to enjoy the cocktail lounge and piano room. Downstairs, there's even a wine cellar for high-end dinner parties.

Besides all that, boaters love having a luxury hotel right on the water where they can stay when they're in Bellingham. Being able to dock their boats right at the hotel is the icing on the cake.

Quoted in *International Travel Review*, talking about the Hotel Bellwether, I said, "It was a perfect setting for a hotel of this nature. I had a dream to put a hotel here and capture the views and the beauty of the water and the harbor... As a result, we have the Hotel Bellwether."

I owned the hotel for ten years and operated it myself. I hired a general manager who had previously been a manager at the RitzCarlton in Phoenix. That manager worked under my supervision and ownership. I was involved every day at the hotel. I had an office right next door, and I paid close attention to the operation of the hotel.

"Mr. Paulsen was very hands-on," Shirley remembers. "He was in Bellingham frequently, running this hotel. The whole community knew Mr. Paulsen, and when he was in town, you'd hear the buzz:

'Yay, Mr. Paulsen is in town!' He knew local politicians and the CEOs of all the companies here." She goes on, "You could go into the Hotel Bellwether's restaurant, and he'd be chatting up the chef, the wait staff, and the host. He treated everybody with enormous kindness."

My daughter, Susan, says, "My dad would do whatever it took to keep things going and on track. One winter, there was unexpected snow. Dad got in his Yukon and drove around Bellingham, picking up stranded maids so that they could make it in to work."

Back in Phoenix, I still had a house, the shopping centers, and some office buildings, but I spent much of my time during this period living on my farm in Bellingham. This way, I was close by and could be at the hotel pretty much daily.

Honestly, this is an example of using a business concern to also follow your heart's desires. I loved Phoenix, and I still love it. But there's always been something about Bellingham that's captivated me. It's a beautiful, special place, and I wanted to spend as much time there as I could.

As I'm sure you've surmised by now, I don't like to be idle. Having a wonderful business enterprise like the Hotel Bellwether gave me true purpose in Bellingham. It gave me the best of both worlds, personal and professional.

SELLING THE HOTEL

After ten years, I was approached by an investor from Vancouver who loved the hotel so much, he wanted to buy it from me. I said, "It's not for sale."

He came back every couple of weeks and continued to ask if he could buy it. Finally, I said, "Okay, make me an offer I can't refuse."

To my surprise, he did just that. He made me an excellent offer, and we reached an agreement for the hotel and the office building (which also includes the ballroom for the hotel). The Port commission also had to approve assigning the lease to the new owner, which they did.

In 2010, I sold the entire property. That Vancouver investor still owns the hotel, but in 2013, the Port bought the office building. The new owner of the hotel wanted to sell the office building, and because the Port already owned the sister office building, they decided to buy this one, too. It's worked out well for the Port because the private sector built it, but now the Port owns it. The office building has performed very well for them.

Since I wouldn't have business dealings in Bellingham anymore, I decided in 2010 that I'd sell my Bellingham farm, too. At that point, I moved to Phoenix full time. (At first, I'd been in Phoenix part time; then it was full time.) I was a little bit sad about that, but overall glad I'd had all those years up there. As I said, it's a very special place, near and dear to my heart.

THE PENINSULA TODAY

Over the years, the 20-acre peninsula where I built the Hotel Bellwether has continued to develop. According to Shirley, "Now there's a huge restaurant, the hotel, two huge office buildings, and three more buildings, offices and apartments, that were later built out there by a different developer."

Shirley goes on, "It's fully built out. There are probably 150,000 square feet of office space, plus the hotel and apartments. It's an enormous job generator down there. Even today, one additional new project is in the works. Not long ago, I called Shirley and told her I had established a foundation for charitable giving, called the Peter Paulsen Foundation. I was looking for ideas about where I could make donations in Bellingham via my foundation.

Shirley gave me a few ideas for nonprofit entities, including Skookum Kids, PeaceHealth St. Joseph Medical Center, and Whatcom Hospice.

Then I asked, "How are things going at the Port?"

"They're going really good," she replied. "We're getting ready to build an event stage on our waterfront." She paused, then said, "Look, it wouldn't really be a donation, but if you paid for the stage, we'd call it the Peter Paulsen Event Stage."

"I'll do it," I said.

The plan is to have community events, concerts, and other performances on the Peter Paulsen Stage. The Port is using my donation to build the stage and bring in ample power for light and sound systems. I'm looking forward to hearing more about it as the Port develops this wonderful project. And I'm thrilled to be donating the funds to make it happen.

"Mr. Paulsen has been such a strong supporter for Bellingham," Shirley says. "He's been very generous to our community. If it wasn't for him, that area wouldn't be what it is today. He was instrumental in turning the peninsula from an underutilized, overgrown site into a beautiful area for all to enjoy."

CHALLENGE YOURSELF

- Have you ever looked around your community and observed a need that isn't being met? Is there a way to turn this need into a business opportunity?

- Consider your business relationships. How long did they take to cultivate? How can you use long-term positive business relationships to your advantage?

- Think about your negotiating skills. Do you generally get what you want? Do you feel you meet others' desires while getting your own met, as well? If not, what steps could you take to improve your negotiating skills?

- What projects that you've completed are you particularly proud of? What features do these projects share?

CHAPTER 16
THE MARKET

FROM BRICKLAYER TO STOCK INVESTOR

Ever since the early days of my success, when I began to have extra savings to work with, I've always invested in the stock market. But after selling the Bellwether Hotel, I became

much more heavily involved in stocks, and investing in futuristic ideas and futuristic companies. It became less of a side project, instead turning into my main focus and the primary usage of my time.

Not long ago, I realized I've gone from bricklayer to home developer, then commercial real estate developer and owner, banker, and from there to shopping center and hotel developer and owner. Now, I was and am a stock investor.

To me, this underscores the importance of reinventing yourself, over and over, especially if you want to be an entrepreneur. Some folks are perfectly happy doing the same job for decades, but many others find themselves burned out or in a rut if they never make any changes. If you want to be an entrepreneur, it's vital that you continually think about how you can adapt. Being adaptable serves you well as the world changes and progresses, and as you age, too. No one stays young forever, but all of us have the capacity to continue using our minds with the energy, intensity, and flexibility of a young person— for as long as we're able.

RESEARCH TO FIND THE BEST ADVICE

When I started investing, I used a stockbroker. But I was quickly unsatisfied with this methodology (by now, this probably doesn't surprise you), because by using a broker, I gave up a lot of control. I wanted to do things my way, the way I've always done new things: by reading and researching, then trusting my own instincts and making my own decisions.

I did extensive reading about how to purchase, own, and (on rare occasions) sell stocks. I listened to what Warren Buffett had to say. In my opinion, Warren Buffett is one of the wisest stock-investing gurus in the world. And one of the key things Buffet says is to buy stocks for the long term to create wealth.

Another thing I learned early on is that in addition to putting my own millions of dollars into stocks, I could borrow more millions of dollars and invest those, too. You can leverage 50% of the value of your stock portfolio. That means if you put in $10 million of your own money, you can borrow another $10 million and invest that, too. This allows you to buy $20 million worth of stocks. By doing this, and by careful research into what stocks to buy, I was able to increase my portfolio many times over.

The stocks I buy are all futuristic thinking. I look for stocks that pay high dividends, and then I hang on to them for the long term.

My advice? Don't be a stock trader. Don't buy for today and sell tomorrow. The only way you make money, Buffet says, is to buy for the long term. I agree with him completely.

Another tip I picked up by reading Buffet is this: don't over diversify. When you diversify too much, it's called indexing. It's better to only invest in A+ rated companies that pay dividends and create good value for long-term investment rather than invest in a wide range of companies, many of which might turn out to be poor investments. You do not want to invest in companies that don't have the potential to make long-term gains.

I follow both pieces of advice. I invest in solid, good companies. That doesn't always mean old, established companies, but it does mean companies who are solid in what they're doing and how they're doing it.

For example, early on, I bought Intel, and Apple, and AT&T. I liked the looks of those companies, liked their models. At the time, they weren't doing as well as they did later, but that worked to my advantage. I bought stock in companies like that when it was selling at fifty cents on the dollar. During the downturn of 2009, I had just sold my office buildings and shopping centers, and numerous good-quality companies were selling at fifty cents on the dollar. So, I invested in stocks in those good-quality companies, which also pay dividends.

Because I borrowed so much money, my interest rate was very low. During the first ten-year period I was seriously investing in stocks, the interest for my loans that I was taking for my stock portfolio were below one percent.

I bought stocks on margin. Essentially, a margin is a loan. For example, you borrow from Charles Schwab, and it's just like a loan. Because I own high-quality stocks, I have never received a margin call. This only happens when an investor has borrowed money to purchase the stock. A margin call occurs when the stock value falls below a certain level. I won't get a margin call unless the margin reaches 70% (which, with the high-quality stocks in my portfolio, has never happened). If you are a beginning investor, I would not recommend buying on margin.

The companies I was buying were paying 7%-8% dividend. Their value had dropped 40%-50%, and the dividend payment did not change. But before I bought, the dividend had been 5%. The stocks split, but the dividends stayed the same, if the company was in a good financial situation.

SHOULD *YOU* USE A BROKER?

You probably already know my answer to this one. In the beginning, I was using a stockbroker from Merrill Lynch. They charged me a fee of about five or ten cents a share. Sounds small, but when you realize how many stocks you purchase at one time, it becomes wildly expensive.

In addition, I was getting advice from the stockbroker that I didn't think was particularly good. I realized that I was better off doing my own thinking and my own investing. I opened an account with Charles Schwab, and everything runs through that. I don't use a stockbroker anymore. I just keep track of everything myself. With the push of a button, I can buy stocks without the influence of a broker.

Don't get me wrong: brokers are fine. A good broker will help you invest in big companies and big mutual funds. But those are prominent brokers, and for providing this service, they make huge sums of money.

Is investing on your own the choice for every investor? Is it the choice for you? I can't answer that because it's an individual decision. It depends on:

- How much money you want to make in stocks
- How much time you're willing to invest in doing the research
- How much risk you're willing to take on

There's no right answer for every investor. I can only tell you what works for me.

MY DAYS AS AN INVESTOR

Currently, I'm spending three or four hours a day on the computer, doing work related to my stock portfolio. I stay on top of everything. If a stock takes a discount and has a temporary setback, I buy more of the stocks I already have. I do that because with the types of companies I invest in, I know it's a temporary low, and I always hold a stock for the long term. This methodology wouldn't work well if you were trading stocks every day or week.

Here's an example: when my two youngest children, Peter and Lauren, were toddlers, I bought stocks for them for their future educations. I put these stocks aside in a "gift to minors" account.

What did I buy? I bought $20,000 worth of Apple, at $1.50 a share. This was in the early 1990s, after Steve Jobs left Apple. As we all know, Jobs came back eventually, and Apple really took off. After many, many stock splits, that $20,000 is now worth $1.5 million. That's about 7,400% profit—until the stocks are cashed in, of course, and taxes need to be paid on that profit.

As it turned out, we didn't cash in those stocks for Peter and Lauren's educations. They still own it. They're no longer minors, so that stock is in their names. It was an investment in their futures, and it paid off big.

But it might not have happened at all. Why? Because the first time the Apple stock split, back when I was still using a stockbroker, my broker told me, "You doubled your money. You should sell that Apple stock."

"No," I replied. "I'm holding long term."

After that first stock split, Apple stock doubled in value many times. That's what I'm talking about: long-term investments are good investments.

Another reason to hold? If you sell too early, you're required to pay income tax. Why not let that tax liability ride, buy more of the same, and create a bigger balance?

SO WHEN *SHOULD* YOU SELL?

This is a great question. I can only answer for myself, but my rule is that I only sell when and if the stock loses its fundamental.

What does that mean? Basically, the fundamental takes into account any information that could potentially impact a stock's price or perceived value. This includes things like:

Cash flow

- ROA: Return on assets, or a ratio of how profitable a company is in comparison to its total assets

- Gearing: The ratio of a company's debt to its equity

- Profit retention and growth investment: How well the company has historically retained profits for funding future growth

- Asset management: How well the company oversees its assets

For example, in 2008, when the market crashed, I had a fair amount of equity in the stock market. But all my stock investment was down 50%. I sold the stocks, which booked a tax loss. Then I sold all my real estate, which had a huge gain. The real estate gain was mostly offset by the loss in stocks, thus mitigating my tax liability.

Thirty-one days later, I bought my stocks back at fifty cents on the dollar. This is an example of why it's important to understand not only a stock's fundamental, but also the tax code.

If you invest on your own, like I do, tracking the fundamental for each company you hold stock in takes a lot of time and a lot of research. But it's vital if you want to manage your own portfolio. You need to know when the fundamental is no longer strong. When that happens, it's probably time to sell.

But if the fundamental is in place and the company looks good for the future, then why sell? Why not just buy more?

FUTURISTIC TECHNOLOGY

How do I figure out which companies to invest in? Remember that "pleasure reading" I mentioned earlier? Using those sources—*The Wall Street Journal*, *Forbes*, *Fortune*, *Financial Times*, and others—I read about what's going on with companies all over the nation. I get a lot of ideas via reading these sources daily, cover to cover. Using these sources, I learn about the future plans of forward-thinking companies.

Like Warren Buffett says, to make big money, you need to invest and hold for the long term. The piece I'd add to that is, I make it my point to invest in futuristic technology.

So, what is futuristic technology?

In my view, it's technology that will be commonplace ten, twenty, or thirty years down the road. An example is electric windmills. Electric windmill technology is dominated by General Electric, so I invest in General Electric.

Another example is electric cars. You might think, here in 2021, that would mean I'd invest in Tesla. But I don't. Why? Because Tesla stock is much too expensive. Also, Tesla is selling at 350 times their P/E ratio. To put that in perspective, General Motors sells at 12 times their P/E ratio.

Tesla is wildly popular right now. Everybody's buying Tesla, and that's why it's so expensive.

I believe Tesla could be a bubble. A lot of people continue buying Tesla, and it's doubled many times. But I don't take that kind of risk. I only buy stocks that actually pay a dividend, and Tesla does not.

Another company I often get asked about is Amazon. It certainly looks like it has a good future. People are buying everything online, much of it from Amazon. They even sell groceries now, since Amazon bought Whole Foods. I believe Amazon has a good future, but right now, its stock price is too high for me. When a stock's price is too high for me to justify, I don't buy it.

Following are some of my major investments and their prices, as of this writing (October 13, 2021):

- Apple 140.91
- IBM 140.76
- Exxon Mobil 61.07
- Qualcomm 125.04
- Intel 52.26
- Microsoft 296.31
- Citibank 78.26
- Ford Motor Co 15.51
- Dow 56.15
- Broadcom 485.01

British Petroleum 29.19 (Note: British Petroleum is heavily invested in green energy; they spend billions of dollars on wind power, solar power, and hydrogen power.)

If you want to make big returns, you need to be in tech and metaverse stocks: companies like Apple, Microsoft, Google, IBM, Qualcomm, Nvidia, and Facebook. They are all up 50% in the last twelve months. Remember, when you are 50% on margin and a stock is up 50%, then your share is up

100%. That's a good investment!

MAKING MY OWN DECISIONS

As is probably evident from this chapter, stocks occupy much of my brain space these days. But I love investing, and I love making my own decisions about stocks—as I do with everything else.

All my life, I've been an entrepreneur. Why should stock investing be any different from, say, owning an investment property? Just as I didn't want to go into business with others when I owned apartment buildings in Moline, I have no interest in using a stockbroker to manage my stocks.

Many stockbrokers are knowledgeable, but most of them are not entrepreneurs. They don't have that entrepreneurial mindset. I don't know what stockbrokers are thinking. I don't know what research they're doing.

Brokers might tell me they're smart, but if they were, they probably wouldn't be stockbrokers. They'd be entrepreneurs!

CHALLENGE YOURSELF

- Thinking back on the jobs you've had, at what times did you have to "reinvent yourself"? What changes did you make to achieve greater success?

- If you've had the same job for a long time, but you want to make changes and/or go into business for yourself, what steps can you take to ensure you're ready for such a large change?

- If you own stocks, are you in it for the long term, or are you primarily interested in short-term gains?

- If you invest in the stock market, do you use a stockbroker? If so, are you satisfied with your investments?

- If you're considering managing your own portfolio, how much time do you have available to devote to it? What resources will you use for research? Are you willing to study widely, thoroughly, and daily, to ensure you invest judiciously?

CHAPTER 17
SHOULD EVERYONE DO THIS?

ONE THING AT A TIME

The previous chapter might make you wonder if you should start doing your own stock investing. It's a question I can't answer for you, because you have to assess your own situation and decide what's right for you.

What I *can* say is this: over the years, one thing I've learned is that you can't be great at everything. Additionally, for most people—myself included—it's difficult to excel at more than one large task or occupation at a time.

To be great at something, you've got to live it, breathe it, eat it, and smell it. I did that when I was a bricklayer. I did it as a home and apartment developer, a commercial real estate developer, a bank owner, a shopping center owner, and a hotel owner. And now I do it as a stock investor.

Would I be able to devote this much time to my stocks if I still had my other businesses? The simple answer is no, I would not. Further, if I didn't devote the time to my portfolio that I do, I'm absolutely certain I wouldn't be as successful an investor as I am.

Perhaps some people are capable of greatness in more than one area at a time. But I believe those people are few and far between. Most of us are much more likely to be successful if we keep our focus as single-minded as possible.

TEACH YOUR CHILDREN

I got my kids involved early in the business world. I made sure they understood the ins and outs of whatever business I was involved in at any one time. This was true for Susan, Peter, and Lauren. Because of Veronica's and

Lisa's challenges, learning intricate details about the business world wasn't possible for either of them, but even they always had a pretty good sense of what their dad was up to, businesswise.

I believe it's important to let your kids know what you're doing with your business. That way, they can learn from you and perhaps start their own businesses down the road. Susan, Peter, and Lauren have all done that.

Susan says, "During the time Dad was building the Moorpark office complex, I worked for him. I was in high school, and I did odd jobs in his office and helped the accountant. I learned a lot about business and dealing with the public. This is part of why I got a degree in business with an emphasis in real estate." She goes on, "I also remember sitting with Dad at the bar in the only restaurant at the Port of Bellingham when he first conceived the idea of the hotel. His favorite tools for outlining ideas were a bar napkin and pen. When he had these tools in hand and his mind was working—which it always was—out would come the ideas."

Susan is an "ideas" person, too. She has a very successful career as a realtor. She's always bringing new ideas and insights to her work.

Perhaps this brings up the question: do my kids manage their own stocks? Have I taught them how to do that? I haven't, actually, and the reason is, by the time I got heavily involved in stock investing, all my kids were adults, with their own occupations and priorities. At this point in their lives, they don't have the time to devote to managing a stock portfolio. Peter Andreas started a meadery wine business in Talent, Oregon, called Steamworks Meadery. Lauren started an organic bakery called Lilac Bakery. So, I manage their stocks for them. Susan is capable of doing most of her own investments, but she calls me from time to time for advice.

The same holds as true for your kids as for you: no one can be great at everything, and people succeed when they put most of their energy into one thing, whatever that one thing is. If you teach your children well, and they turn out to have different passions and interests than you but they're still successful, then you've done your job as a parent.

A HUNDRED PERCENT OF MY TIME

In case you're wondering, yes, I *do* eat and sleep, just like everyone else. I make sure to take time for relaxation. But I still only do one thing at a time. I pay attention to the hotel business, the banking business, the development business, or now the stock business. A hundred percent of my time during my waking hours (and sometimes in the night) is devoted to thinking, thinking, thinking—every day.

This is, again, why I don't use a stockbroker. Yes, stockbrokers are thinking about stocks all the time, too. But they have multiple clients. It would be impossible for any stockbroker to think about my portfolio or yours a hundred percent of the time. Additionally, they work on a commission basis. If you, as the client, don't buy and sell, then your stockbroker doesn't make a commission. Their primary motivation, therefore, is sales: buying and selling stocks.

I moved my accounts to Charles Schwab because they don't charge a commission when you're not using the input from their stockbrokers. I pay no commissions and I don't want input from their stockbrokers, or any other stockbrokers.

As mentioned earlier, I follow the financial news. Every day, I watch CNBC, which is a financial channel. If you want to manage your own portfolio, I highly recommend watching CNBC daily. Once you watch it long enough, you get a feel for what's going on. CNBC features numerous high-end investment gurus, as well as owners and CEOs of companies giving interviews. This is a great way to learn about companies and potential investments, especially futuristic technologies, which I explained in Chapter 16.

It doesn't hurt that Warren Buffett is often on CNBC. I continue to learn so much from him.

That said, you also have to read between the lines. The information on CNBC and from other sources gives you something to think about and something to research. But they're not going to tell you what to do with your stocks—which ones to buy or sell, when to sell, when to hold. You must develop a feel for it and trust your own instincts.

When it comes to stocks, this is my philosophy:

- Buy for the long haul

- Buy good companies with good fundamentals

- Buy stocks that pay a dividend

- Hold unless the fundamentals are no longer there

MAKING IT LOOK EASY

When I look back at myself, at what I've done and what I continue to do, sometimes I'm amazed. But for me, it's easy. It just flows to me.

There's no magic in that, however. The reason it's easy for me is because I study it to the hilt. With regards to stocks, everything I do is easy because I have so much knowledge about it, because I study it so extensively.

Before I invest in a company, I make it a point to learn everything about that company, inside and out. This level of research takes a lot of time. If you're going to study companies extensively, it doesn't make sense to do that for a large number of companies. This is one of the reasons I have a lot of money invested in only about two dozen companies.

Here's what I do:

• Invest heavily in good companies.

• Do not diversify too much. When you diversify, you lose the opportunity to make big money.

• Concentrate on investments and companies that have good fundamentals.

• If you like the fundamentals going forward, then stick to those investments.

Another point about indexing (i.e., diversifying): when you index, some banks want you to be in index stocks. That means they don't have to take a chance. You can't lose any money doing that, but you're not going to make much money, either.

I believe I'm smart enough and thorough enough in my research to anticipate who the winners are, without having to index. Using what I've learned and continue to learn, I concentrate on companies like Intel, Qualcomm, IBM, Broadcom, Microsoft, Apple, and General Electric.

I've also invested in Exxon Mobil and British Petroleum. For these, I doubled my money in the last twelve months. Oil stocks had lost 50% of their value, but now they're getting back to where they were. The low one year ago was $14.74, and as of October 2021 it's at $29.00.

Another point on this: when I bought Exxon Mobile stock, I was getting 11% dividend on the stock. This is because the stock was so cheap that the dividend increased to 11%, and the company never cut the dividend. Exxon Mobile was down 50% from twelve months ago and since then has doubled in value.

I invested heavily into energy stocks that paid a healthy dividend, and it has also doubled in value. The reason the Exxon Mobile stock was down in value one year ago was because of a glut of oil on the market, with no place to store it. I determined Exxon Mobile and British Petroleum are two good companies to invest in. I predicted that oil would return to a high price soon—which it did. Exxon Mobile doubled in September 2021.

In the future, I believe they'll raise the dividend. The stock is now paying about 7% dividend, which is still good enough for me.

When I bought British Petroleum, it was paying 10% dividend. Soon afterward, they cut the dividend. They had been paying 12%, but they cut the dividend in half to 6%. That's still okay with me, so I'm still adding to British Petroleum.

There Are Always Exceptions

I've been asked if I read a company's annual report to gain insight about the company. I do read these reports, but remember, an annual report just tells you where the company has been. I'm much more interested in where they're going. The financial report tells me the fundamentals were in place last year. It tells me if the profit/earnings ratio is in line. But it doesn't tell me where the company is going next year.

I don't labor over a company's 10-Ks and their regular filings. Again, I'm concentrating on where they're going, not where they've been.

One telling feature about a company: does it pay dividends? When the company pays a dividend, that means they have enough cash to give some back to the shareholders. To me, that's one indicator of a solid company.

So, are there exceptions to my rules? Sometimes. For example, I made an exception with Nvidia. I bought that about two years ago and doubled my money, because Nvidia recently made a turnaround. They came out with new technology.

Why did I make that exception? It's because of what I learned through my research. Numerous times on CNBC, I've seen their CEO interviewed. I became intrigued, so I did research on the company and its future. Nvidia designs GPUs (graphics processing units) and SOCs (system on a chip).

Nvidia has a turnaround story. Some time ago, I saw that turnaround coming. I read about the future of Nvidia and kept it on my mind, and that's when I decided to invest in them. I bought stock in Nvidia two years ago, and I've doubled my money there.

Another question I've been asked is, why do I invest in AT&T instead of Verizon? They're both in the telecommunications industry.

They both have phones with the same 5G technology. In many ways, they're very similar.

By now, you've probably deduced the reason: with AT&T, I get 7% or 8% dividend. With Verizon, I'd only get 4% dividend. So for me, that's a no-brainer. They're both good companies, but the dividend made the difference for me.

When you have a lot of money in stocks, and you're weighing the difference between two companies working with the same technologies, a dividend percentage difference like that means your income can increase substantially, just by buying one company rather than the other. There's my answer, right there. It's notable that AT&T owns DirecTV, which is expected to merge with Discovery Channel at the beginning of 2022. At that time, AT&T will sell DirecTV and will most likely cut the dividend.

In all the above examples, the point is the same: *do your research*. Yes, you can make exceptions—*if* you have a good reason. When you're weighing two choices, whether stocks or anything else, consider which brings the greater advantage. Sometimes it might seem like two things are exactly equal, but that's rarely the case. When you research thoroughly, someone or something always emerges as the frontrunner.

AN APPLE GUY

I'm a huge fan of Apple, both investment-wise and as a user of their products. I'm loaded to the hilt on Apple stock; it's one of the biggest holdings in my portfolio. I actually quit buying Apple about a year ago, because I have so much of it. But until then, I was constantly buying Apple.

I have an iPhone. I'm wearing an iWatch, and I work on a Mac. I love my iWatch. It gives me instant messaging, and I can use it to answer a call if my phone isn't nearby.

"Can you hear me okay?" I'll ask the caller. "Yes," they always reply. "Loud and clear."

That technology is phenomenal. That's why I like Apple. I think Apple's future is extraordinary, and I can't wait to see what they come up with next.

I'm a textbook example of the importance of keeping up with technology. Even at this point in my life, after many decades on this planet, I still love technological advances, innovation, and change. I think it's one of the things that keep me young.

A LOT OF GOOD COMPANIES OUT THERE

You can't go wrong with Costco. You can't go wrong with Walmart, Amazon, and Google. I should have owned Costco; I kind of regret now that I didn't buy Costco stock a long time ago. I think it had to do with the dividend. Back then, they probably didn't pay one. I don't know if they pay a dividend now, but they've done so well, it might not have mattered, like it doesn't matter with Nvidia. But you can't win them all.

Long ago, I bought Microsoft stock. I'm as big a believer in Microsoft as I am in Apple. They've been around forever; nonetheless, I think of Microsoft as one of my "futuristic technology" companies. Again, I really look forward to seeing what they do next.

Honestly, there are a lot of good companies out there. You just have to do your research and maintain your focus. I can't emphasize enough the importance of creating a modestly sized portfolio of great companies, knowing everything about them, and holding them for the long term.

Instead of jumping all over the place, I'd rather put my money in a company that I know is forward thinking, is paying dividends (with some notable exceptions), and has solid fundamentals. By following this strategy and devoting countless hours to research, I've managed to double the value of my portfolio every two or three years, to the tune of millions of dollars.

CHALLENGE YOURSELF

What are you great at? What do you love to do most?

If you're not making money doing the thing you love most, is there a way to shift gears to follow your passion *and* be more successful?

If you have children, how much do they know about your work? Have they been to your workplace? In what ways can you teach them what you know, to help prepare them for their own future careers?

Do you have the time and desire to manage your own stock portfolio? If you're considering it, think carefully about your expectations.

Which leaders (whether public figures or people you know personally) do you most admire? Whose advice do you follow regularly and faithfully? What qualities draw you to these individuals?

If you have hard-and-fast rules (personally, professionally, or both), do you ever make an exception? Think about the times you've bent your rules. Was your reasoning solid? Did the exception achieve the goal you wanted? If not, reconsider your rules. Think about when, if ever, might be an applicable time to make an exception, taking into account both the potential risks and rewards of doing so.

CHAPTER 18

GIVING BACK

A LONGTIME GOAL

In addition to my work and investment goals, for about ten or fifteen years, I had another goal: to someday have enough money to establish my own foundation.

A friend of mine in San Jose, John Sobrato, along with his wife, Sue, and their children, manage the Sobrato Family Foundation. Sobrato began his career in real estate. His mother, Ann, was an early real estate entrepreneur in the area; in fact, she's sometimes called the "Mother of Silicon Valley." Like me, John went on to do commercial development. John's real estate and development firm builds on a grand scale, including custom projects for such clients as Lockheed Corporation, Apple, and Netflix. By 2006, his firm had $5 billion in assets. In the 1990s, John and his family started the Sobrato Family Foundation, giving millions to nonprofits, many of them in Silicon Valley.

Hewlett-Packard had a similarly humble start. In 1939, in a onecar garage in Palo Alto, two young men, Bill Hewlett and David Packard, began producing testing and measurement equipment. They built one achievement upon another and were the cofounders of the wildly successful technology company Hewlett-Packard. That garage, by the way, is now an official California Historical Landmark. I have great admiration for people like Sobrato, Hewlett, and Packard. They are (or were, in their lifetimes) extremely wealthy and incredibly smart. I admire anyone who starts with nothing, is innovative, and uses their skills and smarts to build a great company or companies and acquire wealth.

I especially admire anyone who does all that and then gives back by starting a foundation. Seeing this dynamic in action, I always thought, *someday I want to do that.*

Three years ago, this goal was achieved, when I started the Peter Paulsen Foundation.

MANAGING A FOUNDATION

Before starting my foundation, I did what I always do: I researched the subject thoroughly. I wanted to know what was involved in starting a foundation, how to manage it, and how to keep it going. I knew I'd have to manage it on my own, so I wanted to learn everything I could about how to do that.

If you own a company like Hewlett-Packard, you're so huge, you have your own management team for your foundation. I don't know for sure, but I'd guess Bill Hewlett and David Packard never managed their own foundation.

But a management team takes a lot of capital. You have to pay people, of course. You have to give them office space, computers, and equipment. You must make sure they have access to professional learning, to keep up with what's going on in the foundation world. All of that takes money.

My foundation isn't big enough to justify spending that kind of money on a management team. It's just me with input from my wife, Diana. But just because we can't give on the scale that a huge company does, that's no reason not to give at all.

In my view, whenever you have the opportunity to give back, at whatever level is feasible for you, it's a win-win. The beneficiaries of your giving receive the resources they need to keep their nonprofit thriving and helping others in need. And you get the satisfaction of knowing you're doing what you can to help people live better lives.

Currently, I put $1 million to $2 million a year into the Peter Paulsen Foundation. From there, we distribute it to different nonprofits. I use a donor advisory fund (DAF) to manage the funds. The DAF I use is called the Arizona Community Foundation. It's all handled through the Charles Schwab donor advisory program. I deposit money into the DAF and immediately get a receipt for the funds I put in. They keep it for me until I tell them to distribute it where I want it to go. They do all the paperwork, all the bookkeeping, and the tax paperwork, which means I don't have to deal with any of that. I keep the Peter Paulsen Foundation to a manageable size because I want to have intimate knowledge of what's going on. A couple of times a year, I put together a list on my computer of potential organizations to receive funds from the Peter Paulsen Foundation. Then Diana and I go over the list, and we use the Arizona Community Foundation's website to let them know where we want the money to go and how much should go to each organization.

FUNDING A NEED

I give to organizations that need the money and to help the underprivileged. It's a simple philosophy, really. Of course, in order to continue functioning, every nonprofit needs money. I also look for organizations that speak to needs I find relatable.

For example, there are affiliates of the Boys & Girls Clubs of America in cities and towns all over the U.S. They operate afterschool programs, providing a safe and educational place for children and youth to spend their afternoons and evenings. They started as the Boys Clubs of America, and they added "& Girls" in 1990.

Way back in my Moline days, I used to give generously to various needy programs. I did that because I had been a kid without a dad, a kid whose mother worked hard and who myself had to work hard from a very early age. There's nothing wrong with hard work, but if I could help a kid have some fun times in a safe, positive environment—and I could help take the burden off the kid's parents by supporting an organization that provides somewhere that kid can go after school while the parents worked—that felt like a win-win to me.

The Boys Club of Moline (now the Boys & Girls Club of Moline) has a place in my heart, and I still support them. These days, I also give to the Boys & Girls Club of the Valley (Phoenix) and the Boys & Girls Clubs of Whatcom County (Bellingham), as well as other affiliates of the national nonprofit. I've also donated generously to food banks in Bellingham, San Jose, Phoenix, and other locations. I've donated to the Lions Club, particularly to assist with their wheelchair program. I've also supported Goodwill and the Salvation Army. Over the years, I've given a lot of money to organizations that help the disabled, particularly children and the mentally disabled. Not everybody understands issues like cerebral palsy, but it's a very difficult situation for an affected child, the child's parents, and affected adults. I know about it because I studied and learned about it over the years.

Organizations that help the disabled need all the financial assistance they can get, and I'm happy to provide it where I can. Again, this is personal: when my daughters needed help, there were programs available for them. Veronica, for example, went to a day program when she lived in Montecito. She did the most beautiful artwork in her program. At the Santa Barbara Mission, local artists would take the artwork of another artist and replicate it in chalk on the grounds of the mission. One time, they replicated a painting of Veronica's in chalk. She's also had her art hanging in a gallery near the water in Santa Barbara.

That kind of thing wouldn't have happened if Veronica hadn't been in such a wonderful day program. That program did a great job supporting adults who needed extra care. Causes like that are worthwhile, and you can feel good about supporting them.

Some other favorite nonprofits of mine include:

- **The Mayo Clinic (Phoenix).** This nonprofit medical facility focuses on integrated care, education, and research. I have a great deal of respect for the work done at the Mayo Clinic. I give about $500,000 to Mayo every year.

- **The Hope Foundation.** This organization focuses on raising funds to help the disabled—again, a cause that's personally important to me. Last year, I gave $100,000 to the Hope Foundation.

- **Lions Club.** This is a service club that works both within communities (there are 46,000 local clubs throughout the world) and across international borders, with the goals of understanding, civic engagement, and fellowship among people everywhere.

- **Cause4Paws.** This pet food bank provides pet food for people who can't afford to buy it. They also bring pet food to lowincome seniors and veterans, via Meals on Wheels. I'm providing warehouse space for this organization's pet food distribution center.

- **PeaceHealth St. Joseph's Medical Center.** This is a hospital in Bellingham. Because I spent so many years in Bellingham and built the hotel there, I want to give back in that community. Over the years, I've donated $500,000 to PeaceHealth St. Joseph's Medical Center. Recently, I committed to donating $50 million for a new building at PeaceHealth St. Joseph's. The new building will be called the Paulsen Pavilion.

- **Whatcom Hospice.** Again, this is a Bellingham area medical facility. Hospice is so important for end-of-life care, and I donate to support this need in the Bellingham area. I've given

$100,000 to Whatcom Hospice.

CRITERIA FOR GIVING

Of course, I always make sure any organization I give to has 501(c)

(3) nonprofit status. I make sure they qualify from the IRS to receive charitable funds.

I do not give to organizations where most of their money goes to management. With the Boys & Girls Club, it all goes to the cause. It's mostly managed by volunteers, so they don't have a lot of overhead. I know that when I give to them, at least 95% of what I give goes to support programming for kids.

I give generously to the Mayo Clinic every year. They might be slightly over my threshold for management costs, but they're a big

organization with a lot of moving parts, and they do great work. In my view, it's worth it. I'm actually having dinner soon with their CEO, Dr. Richard Gray, to discuss donating to their building fund.

Some programs for children's health and mental health issues are financed by the state and the government. But generally, the government doesn't cover all of their costs, so they need help. That's where foundations like the Peter Paulsen Foundation come in.

WHY I GIVE

My brother, Werner, and I were always taught that, despite the war and the loss of our father, we had a good family life, one for which we should be grateful. Our mother taught us that when you have more than you need, you should contribute and help others. We didn't have money to give away, but we always helped other people by giving food, giving of our time (such as helping out on neighboring farms), and in any other way we could.

We were raised to be helpful to others. That stuck with me for the rest of my life. That's the way I've always tried to live my life, and it's the way I still am today.

My philosophy for the Peter Paulsen Foundation is based on those early life lessons. I'm grateful I learned them, and I'm blessed to be in the position I'm in today, one in which I can use my foundation to lend a helping hand.

I don't believe that you have to be a billionaire in order to donate to worthwhile nonprofits. Yes, many billionaires have foundations and can donate enormous sums of money for the common good.

For an example, here's the timeline of my friend John Sobrato's foundation: https://www.sobrato.com/our-organization/timeline/.

Note the size of some of their gifts: several million dollars. It's wonderful that John and his family are this generous. I admire them greatly for it.

But you know what? No matter what level of contribution you make, every bit helps. If you give at a level that's meaningful to *you*, that's the important thing.

That's my goal with the Peter Paulsen Foundation. By certain standards (certainly those of some of my friends!), my giving is modest at the moment. But my goal is to use my stock investments to grow my contributions to the Peter Paulsen Foundation, over time.

It's the right thing to do. It's what I was raised to do.

CHALLENGE YOURSELF

- Thinking back on your childhood, in what ways was it plentiful?

In what ways did you or your family need more? What resources, if any, helped your family during difficult times?

- What life lessons about giving did you receive as a child, youth, and young adult? How have you incorporated those lessons into your life?

- Who are your heroes? Whose life and work philosophy do you admire, and why?

- If you're in a position to give back, at any level, what organizations do you support? Why do these organizations receive your support?

CHAPTER 19
MY LIFE TOD A Y

ALL ABOUT DIANA

This book is primarily about how I built my businesses and my wealth, with a few side trips into my hobbies and other interests. In this chapter, I'll talk briefly about other aspects of my personal life.

One of the most important people in my life is my wife, Diana, so I'll start by telling you about her.

Diana was born and raised in Bulgaria. She immigrated to the

U.S. in 2000, around the same time I moved to Phoenix. We didn't meet at that time, however. We met about fifteen years later. Diana was working for a buddy of mine, and she and I became friends. After a while, we decided to take our relationship to the next level. And here we are.

We've been married for five years. Diana's European background and education match mine perfectly. Because of my upbringing, I'm very European in my ways of life, and so is she. Like me, Diana took ballroom dance classes in school. She also took gymnastics when she was young. At the age of 18, back in Bulgaria, she trained to be a nurse and a dental assistant. Again, this is like me: just as I did, she followed up her high school years by acquiring the education to have a skilled profession. This is very common for Europeans. Even today, a lot of young Europeans approach their post-high school education in this way.

Diana is an amazing cook and meticulous housekeeper. As do I, she loves to entertain. We often go out to dinner with friends, but we also greatly enjoy having people over. Diana loves cooking for guests.

Like me, Diana was married previously. She has two kids and five grand-kids. Her youngest grandchild was just born this past spring.

My daughter, Susan, says this about Diana: "She's a blessing. When Diana came along, she kind of represented a new beginning for Dad. Being European, she has similar roots to his. He likes things clean and organized, and so does she. A lot of the women he dated prior to Diana wanted servants, and they expected that Dad would want that, too. These women had no interest in taking care of him or helping him, let alone maintaining a house. Even if you have a regular house cleaner, it's still a lot to take care of things on a daily basis—cook, do dishes, keep things organized. Dad likes things tidy and neat, and so does Diana. They're both old school; they do for themselves everything they can."

Susan continues: "Diana is beautiful and smart. She gives Dad what he needs. She complements him and balances his life."

My daughter is right about all of that. Diana and I really are on the same wavelength. I truly enjoy her company, and she enjoys mine. We consider ourselves very fortunate that our paths crossed when they did.

I've had many years of experience with women. I'll admit it, there have been ups and downs in my love life. As Susan mentioned, I dated some women who were wrong for me. And I know I made mistakes in both of my first two marriages.

But what I learned from all that is, you don't give up. If you're single and you'd like to have a life partner, then keep putting yourself out there. Make sure you're meeting people and remaining open to possibilities. Don't give up until the right one comes along. There's somebody out there for everyone. I truly believe that!

HOME STUDY

Everything I do, I study to the hilt. That doesn't just go for business, or for investing in stocks. Even with home ownership, the same principle applies:

study everything, learn everything, and *then* make a decision.

Diana and I just bought a beautiful new house in Phoenix. I built my first house in Phoenix about twenty years ago. I built it from scratch; built it myself. It was 10,000 square feet. But over the years, I determined it was bigger than I needed or wanted. Diana agreed, so a few years into our marriage, we decided to find a new, smaller home. We've downsized to a 5,000-square-foot home.

Before we started looking, we had a lot of discussions about what we wanted in a house. Our goal was to be on the same page, because that would allow us to make a decision we'd both be happy with. We determined the size of house we wanted, and we agreed that we wanted everything in the house to be top of the line.

I look at a house as a long-term investment, and so does Diana. Not just because most homes increase in value if you maintain them and hold on to them long enough. But more than that, a house should bring its occupants a great deal of pleasure. Most of us spend the majority of our time inside our houses, as well as in our back yards and other outdoor spaces attached to our homes. Why not be as comfortable in your home environment as you possibly can be?

The key to that is doing research and research and research. Make sure you know what you're looking for. If you're part of a couple, take the time to iron out any differences of opinion *before* you start looking. Otherwise, one of you will feel you're making too many compromises, and that person will never be happy in the home. Both people should be happy and comfortable.

Everything Diana and I do, we study to the hilt. Diana enjoys doing things this way, too. I'm the businessman, but she's on the same page as far as thinking long term and thinking about high quality. High-quality lifestyle, high-quality projects. She enjoys thoroughly researching what we're doing, same as I do.

I'm more aggressive in my stock research than I am in house hunting, but I apply the same principles to either task. With real estate, we study the ins and outs of it, and we're not too quick to buy anything. This holds true for both a primary residence and a vacation home.

We love Phoenix, but we also have a getaway place in Newport Beach, California. The California state income tax rate is very high, and because of that, we don't want to be California residents. But if we spend less than 180 days a year at our Newport Beach place, it's considered a second home, not a permanent residence. So, we spend our summers there, usually from July to September. It's too hot in Phoenix in the summer, anyway. We'd much rather be near the water in the summertime.

Again, however, when buying our place in Newport Beach, we spent a lot of time researching and talking about what we wanted, before we began house hunting. Eventually, we found the perfect place for us.

If you're in the market for real estate, I highly recommend doing your homework at the start of your search. Don't get caught up in excitement about the first place you see. Especially if you're in a competitive, high-priced market, that's a good way to overpay and to end up with a place that's not right for you. Take your time, put in the research hours, and ensure you're positioned to make a solid, strong offer when the right place comes along.

GETTING AROUND AND GETTING HELP

In previous chapters, I talked about my cars and boats. I still love to drive, but I don't boat anymore. It was wonderful owning boats, and I still enjoy being on the water, but I'm happy not to have the responsibilities of boat ownership anymore.

These days, to get from one far-off location to another (for instance, from Phoenix to Newport Beach, or to northern California to visit Veronica, Susan, and Lisa), we joined the NetJets program. This is a Berkshire Hathaway company that puts a private plane at our disposal anytime we need it. We love that very much. We fly into private airports, and a rental car is waiting for us at the runway when we arrive. When we go home again, we just leave the car at the private airport. It's amazingly convenient.

As for getting help—I do need some, of course. There was a time when I had numerous employees, but now I only have one. Her name is Mary, and she's my part-time secretary. Mary is also a real estate broker. She does a little extra stuff that I need taken care of. Diana helps me a lot, too.

Mostly, though, I do for myself everything I'm able to. I'm not involved in real estate development anymore. It's too time intensive. Now, I'm just having fun working on my investments. And I'm making more money than I ever did before. You can't beat that!

I've had to accept some of the slowing down that comes with age. It's not always easy to do that but keeping your mind sharp and occupied makes a huge difference in your quality of life as a senior citizen. Being gracious about accepting help when you need it also goes a long way toward a fulfilling existence in one's golden years. That doesn't mean you should consider yourself useless, but it does mean safeguarding your energy and time for the things you're most passionate about and that make you happiest.

MY OLDER KIDS: VERONICA, SUSAN, AND LISA

As I've mentioned, Veronica, my oldest daughter, has a disability. Her brain only developed so far on the learning curve. When she was a baby, she had a very high fever, which caused her disability. We didn't know about it until she was in kindergarten. The teachers discovered it. Her abilities as a schoolchild and into adulthood were limited. Her mental development goes to about age eight. But over the years, she's been able to live independently, with the help of caregivers and day programs. These days, she's doing extremely well. I provide for her financially, and she lives about a mile from Susan, in Chico, California. Veronica smiles and is happy every day. She has such a good outlook, and I'm grateful for that.

You've no doubt noticed that my second daughter, Susan, is quoted quite a bit in this book. She and I have always been close, and I believe I've influenced her a lot.

When she was 19, Susan married her high school sweetheart, Gary McEwan. Unfortunately, Gary got leukemia and passed away a year later. After that, I helped Susan buy a little house in San Jose. But soon after, she decided to move to Paradise, California. She sold the San Jose house and bought a cottage in Paradise. She then went to Chico State University, where she studied business and real estate law. She also minored in art; she still works in ceramics and sculpture. Susan has two kids, Heather and Logan. She never married her kids' dad, but they were friends and got along fine. He recently passed away. In 2000, Susan married a man named Rick, on board

the *Freya*, as explained earlier.

She lived in Paradise for over thirty years. In 2007, when Veronica needed more help, she moved to Paradise, too, where Susan picked out a nice house for her. I paid for the house, and Susan got Veronica settled in.

One day, when Susan was working and had Veronica with her in the car, they previewed a house that was coming on the market. As Susan tells it, "A realtor can preview a house literally in about a minute. My dad and I have always enjoyed looking at real estate, and Veronica likes watching those remodeling shows on TV. So this is an interest we all share. That day, I pulled up to a particular house, and Veronica said, 'Oh, Susie, you bought me the wrong house. *This* is my house.'"

The house was on the canyon and abutted a park. It had a huge garage, perfect for Rick. There was a handicap-accessible bedroom. Susan says, "It was just like a gift from heaven."

As it turned out, I helped Susan leverage some money, enabling her to buy that house. I was so happy to be able to do this.

Then, in 2018, the Camp Fire swept through Paradise, destroying over 18,000 structures. Both Veronica's and Susan's houses were lost, and Susan also lost a rental house to the fire. They were lucky to evacuate before the fire got close to them. After that, they moved to Chico, about fifteen miles away.

My third daughter, Lisa, has similar issues to Veronica's, but not as severe. I'm supporting them both, and Susan looks after them. As Veronica says, "Susie knows how to fix things." This is true; Susan is extremely capable. Perhaps it's in our genes, or maybe simply learning the right life lessons. I learned from my mother how to be capable, and in turn, I taught Susan.

On her own level, Lisa is capable, too. She can drive a car and has been married. She had a son, Christopher, with her first husband, but they divorced, and his parents mostly raised Christopher. With her second husband, she had a daughter, Tabitha. Although Tabitha had a difficult childhood, she's grown into an amazing young woman and has a new baby herself. Her experience is a good reminder that we all can rise out of hardship.

Susan's daughter, Heather, graduated from Chico State. She's married to a man she met in college, and they have two young kids. The kids are amazingly smart and beautiful. I've set up an education fund for them so they can go to college someday.

Logan, Susan's son, is single. About her son, Susan says: "Logan is a Gemini like my dad, very charismatic. He speaks German, and he recently bought a house in Chico."

When we go to Chico to visit everyone, we often charter a private plane from NetJets. For those visits, Susan gets the whole family together. That way, I can see them all at once, at Susan's house.

I hope my daughters have learned from me. In their own ways, they continue to teach me, too. That's one of the blessings of living a long life and having adult children. You can learn from each other.

MY YOUNGER KIDS: DREA AND LAUREN

My younger two children, whom I adopted with my second wife, Angela, are both doing great. My son is called Drea (his middle name is Andreas, after my father). A few years ago, he started a meadery. Mead is wine made from fermented honey. It's getting to be the new college drink. Drea is producing mead in Talent, Oregon, not far from Ashland, close to the California border.

Several years ago, my daughter, Lauren, opened a bakery in Poulsbo, Washington. It was all delicatessen food and baked items. She even sold a dessert made from one of my mother's recipes: Zitrone Pudding, a light lemon chiffon pudding made from egg whites and lemon custard. It's like a lemon cloud.

Unfortunately, Lauren had to close the bakery down because of the pandemic. She sold it and moved back to Bellingham. She wants to raise a family and figures Bellingham is a good place for that. I agree with her!

Both Drea and Lauren are entrepreneurs, like me. I love that they're following in my footsteps in this way, and I'm very proud of them.

FAMILY LIFE

All in all, my personal life and family life are truly wonderful. My brother, Werner, is still living in Moline, and I visit him occasionally, as well as seeing other relatives there. I get to fly by private jet to see my kids, grandkids, and great-grandkids whenever I want. I spend my winters in Phoenix and my summers in Newport Beach, California.

Best of all, every day, I get to wake up next to Diana, my wonderful wife.

I feel very blessed.

CHALLENGE YOURSELF

•	If you have a spouse or life partner, what do you love most about that person? How do you make time for each other and appreciate each other?

•	If you're single and want to be partnered, in what ways are you putting yourself out there to meet people?

•	Are you in the market for real estate? If so, what research have you done or do you plan to do, to find the best home for yourself and your family?

•	Do you have children? If so, in what ways have you taught them important life lessons? In what ways do you learn from your children?

•	If you're a senior, how do you keep yourself active and keep your mind sharp? What limitations have you had to accept, and where can you find balance between your limitations and your capabilities?

CHAPTER 20

LOOKING AHEAD

NO SUCH THING AS RETIREMENT

I never really retired. There was never a point where I said, "All right, I'm done."

Honestly, I don't think I'll ever retire. Every day, I'm still looking for opportunities for my stock portfolio. I have no plans to put that aside.

A few years ago, I had cancer. I was fortunate that it wasn't serious, but it caused me to make sure I had my affairs in order. It also made me realize I'm at my best when I take action, push forward, and remain optimistic.

I've accomplished a lot of different things in my life, but the one constant is that I've always been very focused, always done only one thing at a time. When I was young, it was my education. Then it was masonry. Then single-family home development, followed by apartment building development, then commercial real estate development. Then there were the shopping centers, and following those, the hotel. And now it's investing in the stock market. There are a lot of different ways to make a living, and over the years, I've taken on many occupations that appealed to me. But it was always just one thing at a time.

DAILY ROUTINE

I start every day by turning on my laptop, just to see how my stocks are doing. I also check the financial news every morning. I watch CNBC to see what's on the horizon—what ideas are new, what technology is new.

I also watch *Bloomberg* financial news. I watch those programs religiously. I learn what's going on in the world, especially in technology, so I can make good decisions about acquiring additional stocks and making financial investments. When the market has a downturn and stocks are cheaper, I buy more of the stocks I already have.

Every morning, I spend about three or four hours on the computer. In the afternoon, I like to relax. Much of my relaxation time, of course, is spent reading.

In the evening, we often entertain guests or go out to dinner. Diana and I have a good social circle here in Phoenix. We love seeing our friends and meeting new people.

I try to surround myself with bright, interesting people. I think that's another thing that keeps a person young: engaging with others and being interested in the world around you. In this way, you keep from spending too much time inside your own head.

WHAT'S COMING UP?

I'm very much looking forward to the performance stage they're building at the Port of Bellingham, the one which I'm paying for and they're going to call the Peter Paulsen Stage. Shirley McFearin keeps me informed about the progress on this project. It's one of my contributions to Bellingham, and I can't wait to see the finished product. Also in Bellingham, I've worked with PeaceHealth

St. Joseph Medical Center to help them with various programs and expansion.

Diana and I continue to travel whenever we can. The pandemic made travel difficult, but now we're getting out a bit more again. As mentioned, we feel fortunate to belong to NetJets, which makes travel very easy.

I highly recommend traveling if you have the ability and the means to do it. Planning and looking forward to a trip—and then getting to experience the trip itself—is another way to keep your mind focused on what's ahead.

REGRETS?

That's such a loaded word—*regrets*. I don't think it's useful to ruminate on the past. But it's impossible to live as long as I have without having some thoughts of "What if I'd made a different choice?"

On the financial side, I have zero regrets. I made smart business decisions all along, and everything I did paid off.

But looking back on my personal life, I probably worked too hard and spent too many hours wrapped up in my business life. Too much time at the office cost me two marriages, and I didn't spend enough time with my family.

I can't change that, but I'm doing what I can to make up for it now. I'm not working much in the field anymore. Today's technology makes it all so much easier than it used to be. Also, because   all I'm doing now is investing, I don't have to go anywhere. I don't have to go to an office to place my stock orders. I do it all on the internet. I do everything from home, including all my research, every day.

I operate completely on my laptop. Because my work is done remotely, my wife has me at home with her.

Maybe I'm around *too* much! But Diana loves it!

WHAT WILL THE FUTURE BRING?

No matter your age, I think it's important to always have something to look forward to and something to be working toward. My hope for the future is to keep investing in my stock portfolio. It's doubled and tripled a couple of times. I hope it doubles and triples another couple of times, so I can eventually leave a substantial sum to charity. I don't want to leave all the money to my children. Partially because there are so many people in the world who are in desperate need, and partially because I don't think my kids would know what to do with that much money!

I hope to build up a solid, sizeable portfolio of financial assets, so when

I'm gone, I'll be able to leave a significant amount to charity. That's my plan. Along the way, I plan to keep increasing my charitable giving. Next year, I'd like to increase my annual donation from one million to two million dollars, so I can help more people along the way.

I don't need any more money for my lifestyle. We have a wonderful life, Diana and I. We can do whatever we want to do. We don't need to spend and spend and spend. The excess is just building up, and most of it will go to my foundation. That, in turn, will help people who need extra funding because they're in a difficult patch, or in some cases simply for their day-to-day existence.

It's gratifying to know that someday, when I'm gone, that will be my legacy.

ANGELS – AND ATTITUDE

Most of what I set out to do turns out exactly right. Maybe my angels have something to do with it.

But I think the biggest difference is my attitude. Looking back on my life, and even today, not *everything* seems exactly right in the moment. Yes, a lot of things do, but when something happens to me that doesn't seem right, I remind myself that what happened was meant to be. Every time I've done that, something better happens within a short period of time.

For example, when a business deal falls apart, I don't get upset about it, because it's always, without exception, replaced by something better. During my career, that happened to me time and again. It's even true of little things. What if my car won't start, or I get a flat tire? I could get angry about that, but I don't, because I know it happened for a reason. That delay kept me from being somewhere I wasn't meant to be.

For example, years ago when I lived in Hillsboro, one day I was supposed to meet with Sylvia Brown, the world-renowned psychic. We were meeting in San Jose, about a thirty-minute drive from my house. As I exited my property, going through the large iron gate that led to my driveway, the gate closed right on my car. To this day, I don't know why that happened, just some malfunction with the gate. I was fine, but the car wasn't. This was in the days before cell phones, so it took a while to straighten everything out and get to my meeting with Sylvia. When I finally arrived, she said, "Peter, you are late. You're never late!"

When I told her what happened, she said, "Oh, no, Peter! On your brand-new Mercedes? You must have been very upset!"

"Not at all," I replied. "It kept me out of harm's way on my drive to San Jose."

"Oh?" she said.

"Sure," I said. "I never worry. I know that when there's a delay, it happens because I was where I was meant to be, instead of somewhere else."

Sylvia closed her eyes. "So something happened somewhere else. Somewhere you would have been if the gate didn't close on your car." Opening her eyes, she asked, "Is that it?"

"I believe so," I said. "But even if I don't know exactly why, I'm sure there was a good reason."

Sylvia nodded. "I completely agree. Things *do* happen for a reason."

Then I said, "Do you want to hear a story about a time when I

did find out the reason?" "Certainly," she replied.

This is the story I told her: Years earlier, I was in Dallas for a builder's convention. The whole group of builders was meeting up at the Hungry Hunter, a restaurant thirty minutes from downtown Dallas. Four of us grabbed a cab and were on the freeway, in stop-and-go traffic. As the cab driver took the exit to get the restaurant, he said, "Oh, my goodness, sorry. I took the wrong exit. I need to get back on the freeway."

Everyone else in the car was concerned we'd be late to dinner. But I wasn't worried, because I knew that since we'd exited the freeway, there was a good reason for that.

Sure enough, as the cab driver entered the freeway again, we came to an abrupt stop. Turns out a huge accident had just happened, a fifty-car pileup, right where we would have been if we hadn't gotten off at that exit.

So you see, taking the wrong exit was not a mistake. It kept me and all of us in the cab out of harm's way.

After I told Sylvia that story, she smiled. "That is an excellent story," she said. "It illustrates how we can use positive thinking to help us understand why fate, or God, turns matters the way they turn."

Later, Sylvia ended up using that story as an example on her TV show.

THE LORD IS MY SHEPHERD

I've never been an overly religious man, but I do believe in God (and angels!), and I do still follow the teachings of the church, which I learned as a child. When I was growing up in Germany, all children from ages 10 to 14 in our village attended Bible classes at the Lutheran Church and were confirmed at age 14. At confirmation, the pastor bestowed on each one of us a Psalm, printed on our confirmation certificates. Mine was Psalm 23:

The Lord is my Shepherd, I shall not want. He maketh me to lie

down in green pastures: He leadeth me beside the still waters. He restoreth my soul: He leadeth me in the paths of righteousness for His name's sake. Yea, though I walk through the valley of the shadow of death, I will fear no evil: for Thou art with me. Thy rod and Thy staff, they comfort me. Thou preparest a table before me in the presence of mine enemies: Thou anointest my head with oil; my cup runneth over. Surely goodness and mercy shall follow me all the days of my life: and I will dwell in the house of the Lord forever.

I have carried this Psalm with me throughout my life, and it fits me perfectly.

Angels on *Your* Shoulders

Looking back on my life, I've been extraordinarily fortunate. Perhaps Tanta Tieda was right, and I do have angels on my shoulders.

Because I recognize this and never take it for granted, I do what I can to help other people achieve their goals and realize their dreams.

That's my goal—to help people live the best lives they can.

That's what I want for you, too. I want you to feel like you have angels on *your* shoulders!

CHALLENGE YOURSELF

- If you're still working, do you hope to retire someday? If so, what plans (financial and otherwise) are you putting in place to meet your retirement goals?

- Think about your day-to-day routine. Is it rewarding? If not, in what ways might you change things up?

- Do you have regrets? Remember, you can't change the past, but you can learn from it. What can you learn from your past that might change your present and future circumstances?

- What are your short-term goals? What are your long-term goals? What are you most hoping for, and what will it take to help you realize your dreams?

- When things don't seem right at first, can you find the good in how things turn out? Are you able to adjust your thoughts in a positive way, leading toward positive outcomes?

Printed in the USA
CPSIA information can be obtained
at www.ICGtesting.com
CBHW041333011124
16734CB00054B/521

9 798330 248162